REGGAE POET
The Story of
BOB MARLEY

REGGAE POET

The Story of

BOB MARLEY

Calvin Craig Miller

MORGAN REYNOLDS

PUBLISHING

Greensboro, North Carolina

Modern Music Masters

Ray Charles
George Gershwin
John Coltrane
Irving Berlin
John Lennon
Bob Marley

REGGAE POET: THE STORY OF BOB MARLEY

Library of Congress Cataloging-in-Publication Data

Miller, Calvin Craig, 1954-
  Reggae poet : the story of Bob Marley / by Calvin Craig Miller.
    p. cm.
  Includes bibliographical references (p.   ) and index.
  ISBN-13: 978-1-59935-071-4
  ISBN-10: 1-59935-071-8
    1. Marley, Bob--Juvenile literature. 2. Singers--Jamaica--Biography--
Juvenile literature. 3. Reggae musicians--Jamaica--Biography--Juvenile lit-
erature. I. Title.

  ML3930.M315M55 2007
  782.421646092--dc22
  [B]
                                        2007027476

Printed in the United States of America
First Edition

Contents

Bob Marley
(Courtesy of UrbanImage.tv/56 Hope Road Music/Adrian Boot)

one

Nine Miles Boy

The raucous cheers of 80,000 fans greeted reggae superstar Bob Marley when he walked onstage in National Heroes Circle Stadium in Kingston, Jamaica. The cheers didn't stop when the main attraction of the Smile Jamaica Concert told the crowd he would only perform one song. Usually, such an announcement by a top billed performer would invite a chorus of boos. But the throng gathered at Heroes Circle on December 5, 1976, knew this was not a typical concert. They knew Marley was risking his life to play for them.

When politically inspired violence threatened the security of Jamaica's 1976 elections, the politicians turned to Marley for help. It is unusual for politicians to ask musicians to help solve national problems, but Bob Marley was not your average artist. His songs protesting injustice and demanding equality for everyone had inspired a world audience. Within Jamaica, his legend was a source of national pride.

The Smile Jamaica concert had been planned as a way to help unite the country.

Unfortunately, not everyone in Jamaica wanted peace. Two nights before the concert gunmen had broken into Marley's house on Hope Road in Kingston and attempted to assassinate him. They had shot him in the chest and his wife Rita, a singer for the Wailers, was shot in the head. Both of them survived the assault and had retreated to a secret compound in the Blue Mountains.

The shooting had thrown the Wailers' appearance into doubt, but Bob refused to be cowed. The thunderous applause that shook the stadium when it was announced Bob Marley and the Wailers would play that night was the crowd's way of saying they admired and appreciated Bob's courage.

"When me decided to do this yere concert two anna 'alf months ago, me was told dere was no politics," Marley said that night. "I jus' wanted to play fe de love of de people." Then he launched into one of his best known song "War," which was about the violence brought about by inequality.

Enthused by the support of the crowd, Marley and the Wailers didn't leave the stage after one song. Instead they played a ninety-minute set. Rita was on stage singing backup and wearing a scarf to cover the flesh wound in her scalp. As Bob sang, he danced across the stage, shaking his fourteen-inch dreadlocks in defiance. His eyes twinkled mischievously as he made jokes about his would-be assassins.

Despite the attack, Bob Marley fulfilled his promise to Jamaica's leaders by transforming a potentially dangerous occasion into a festival of joy. Just before leaving the stage, he threw his head back and laughed, a gesture of elation and defiance that drew a roar of approval from the crowd.

Bob Marley pioneered Jamaican reggae music, making it popular in both America and Europe. *(Courtesy of AP Images)*

Bob Marley and the Wailers changed Jamaican music and Jamaican society. Before they emerged on the scene, Jamaica's best singers had been poorly paid and little respected. Marley and his band were the first musicians from a developing country to win success with American and European audiences. His songs help to pioneer a new form of music called reggae, which enthralled its devotees with a slow syncopated backbeat that combined rock and soul music. Although he wrote his share of love songs, Marley did more than croon about love or relationships. He sang about poverty, war, and racial strife. He might not have been the first popular artist to sing about social issues, but his appeal transcended many other protest singers. Governments and antigovernment rebels alike recognized the power of his music. African guerrillas waging war against white rule in Rhodesia took his song "Zimbabwe" as an anthem. In 1978, African delegates to the United Nations awarded him the Third World Peace Medal on behalf of "500 million Africans."

Marley wrote songs that expressed serious personal and political issues—social justice, spiritual awakening, compassion—in a clear style that said the deeper truths of life were often very simple. As he said on one occasion, in the mix of African and English slang that made up the Jamaican patois (he spoke in more precise English only when he needed to so that an interviewer could understand), "De trut' is always dere, you got to seek it out, dat's all. Dere is plenty of wisdom on dis earth dat people don't know."

Now a new generation has discovered the wisdom of Bob Marley's music. After his death in 1981, Bob Marley's reputation continued to grow. Posthumous awards, newspaper and magazine tributes, as well as millions of Web pages, give testament to the reverence with which his fans regard him. His native country has designated days in his honor and minted coins stamped with his image.

Trench Town, the area of West Kingston where Bob was raised in the 1950s and 1960s, was one of the poorest places in the Western Hemisphere. Wooden shacks were shoved hovels made of scrap tin and cardboard. Three or four

Bob Marley's childhood Trench Town home *(Courtesy of AP Images/Collin Reid)*

families sometimes lived in a single shack. There was no escape from the heat, not even the refuge available in American ghettos, where people could at least flee temporarily to an air-conditioned store or public building. There were few public facilities and paths and alleys twisted among the fragile shacks. Thieves and gunmen lurked in the trails, waiting to jump the unwary.

As a boy Bob earned the street name "Tuff Gong." It was given to him because of willingness to defend himself in gang fights. He never forgot the lessons of Trench Town.

He never forgot the poor, either, singing of their plight and handing out money to less fortunate friends, long after he no longer had to worry about money.

Bob Marley did not begin his life in Trench Town. His early years were spent in the less threatening tiny village of Nine Miles, which came by its name not for any reason related to its history or people, but as a simple geographical marker: it is situated nine miles from Alexandria, the closest sizable town. Nine Miles was surrounded by good farmland to grow yams, cocoa beans, sugarcane, and corn, as well as an abundance of fruits, including lemons, bananas, grapefruit, limes, and pears. Despite its ample food supply, there were no modern conveniences, such as electricity or running water, in Nine Miles.

Cedella Malcolm, Bob's mother, lived a sparse, simple life working on her father Omeriah's farm. Cedella, or Ciddy as she was called, learned to read and write, but could not tolerate being cooped up in a classroom and quit school at the age of ten. She spent most of her childhood working on the farm. She was in her late teens when she met Captain Norval Sinclair Marley. Norval Marley cut a dashing figure. He worked as an official with the British government, in charge of handing out land to war veterans and pensioners. He would ride through Nine Miles inspecting land on his white horse, seeming quite the romantic figure to young Ciddy. She remembered him as a tall man, but he was in fact only five-foot-five. He was also much older than she, in his early sixties when they met. Nevertheless, they were soon lovers.

Norval Marley was a white man, which added an element of risk to their courtship. Whites in Jamaica were a slim

Bob Marley's mother, Cedella Marley Booker, blows a kiss to the crowd after a performance in this 2005 photo. *(Courtesy of AP Images/Boris Heger)*

minority, but generally held higher social status than blacks. Norval Marley risked scorn and possibly disinheritance from his own family for involvement with a black woman.

Omeriah tried to talk his daughter out of the relationship. Norval was several years older than Omeriah, and he thought Norval was taking advantage of her. But he couldn't change her mind.

At age eighteen she became pregnant and Norval married her. The ceremony was performed on June 9, 1944. The couple fudged a bit on the facts for the official records, with Norval listing his age as fifty and Ciddy claiming she was twenty. But the most controversial part of their union was preserved in the parish register; the bride was listed as black, the groom as white. The mixed marriage of his parents would haunt Bob Marley and cause him to suffer much abuse growing up.

Cedella went into labor during a church service on February 4, 1945. A woman named Auntie Missy acted as midwife through the long and painful labor. The young mother did not understand that she was supposed to push as the baby was being born. She cried out in her pain to Auntie Missy, seeking reassurance. Auntie Missy pointed to pictures of women hanging on the wall. "See all those pictures on de wall of all doze pretty lady? Everyone of dem had to go through what you're going through here."

She rubbed Cedella's belly with oil and commanded her to push. Two days after the pains began, and after many hours of hard labor Cedella's first child was born, on February 6, 1945.

Cedella's family gathered around the bedside to see the new baby. Her sisters wanted to hold and touch him and his grandfather Omeriah was bursting with pride. The baby's arrival also thrilled Norval Marley. He insisted on giving the baby a name his mother at first did not like. Norval wanted the baby be called Nesta Robert Marley. Cedella had never heard of a boy named Nesta, and Norval offered no explanation of where the name came from, saying only that he liked it.

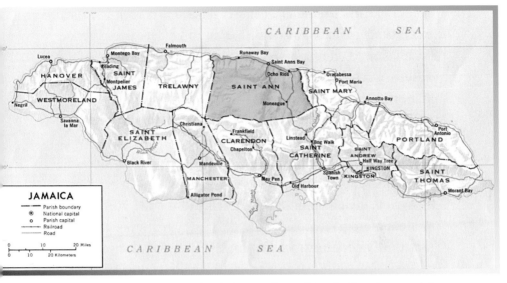

Nine Miles, Bob Marley's birthplace, is located in the Jamaican parish of Saint Ann.

Cedella suggested Lester as a compromise, but she could not persuade the Norval to change his mind. She later learned the word Nesta meant Messenger. Throughout his childhood, Cedella called the boy Nesta, never Robert or Bob.

When Nesta was about four he began to play at the ancient practice of reading palms. Palm readers claim to be able to see a person's future by looking at the wrinkles and creases of their palms. Cedella considered it a child's game, but her neighbors came to believe in the boy's psychic abilities. One of the first to seriously assert that Nesta had the ability to read palms was a local woman called Aunt Zen. When she told Cedella that Nesta had read her fate in her hand, the mother was skeptical. She insisted the boy was only playing.

"Auntie Ciddy, everything Nesta tell me come true!" Aunt Zen said. A local constable, widely respected in Nine Miles, later told Cedella the same thing. Nesta had read his palm and accurately predicted later events. Perhaps unknowingly, Nesta had picked up one of his family traits, a tendency to practice mysticism. Mystics claim to be able to see the nature of an unseen world, including God, through intuition, an ability that brings great power. Nesta's grandfather Omeriah was a *myalman,* one who used herbs and dances to cure the sick by purging evil spirits. The myalmen believed sickness was caused by distress of the soul rather than the body. Their beliefs came from the tradition of the medicine men who practiced in Africa, dancing and chanting to cure the ill. They stood as a counterpart to *obeahmen,* who used their magical gifts for evil. Omeriah was sometimes accused of using obeah, but that was only gossip. Omeriah would use his practices in healing rituals for Nesta when the boy fell ill.

Nesta's palm reading phase did not last long. He began to sing, an activity he considered more satisfying than looking into other people's futures. About the same time, he began his education at the Stepney School in Nine Miles. He soon found he preferred music and athletic games to classroom studies.

It was not that the boy lacked academic ability. He did well enough in reading and arithmetic to tutor other students, but much like his mother he hated being in a classroom. He loved to run and would rather be outside. Recess came as a great relief, a time when he could close his books and join in the soccer games, kicking oranges and grapefruits when they lacked a ball.

Singing grew from a pastime to a passion. Nesta had a soft voice, but it was clear and musical. He won a pound—the equivalent of about two U.S. dollars—at a singing contest at Fig Tree Corner. Nesta was happy in Nine Miles, even though money and sometimes even food were scarce.

His father first took him to the big city of Kingston when he was six. Norval, who no longer lived with his new family, showed up one day and announced he was taking Nesta to boarding school. Cedella was reluctant to see her son go, but Norval persuaded her that it was in the boy's best interest.

Months went by without so much as a brief letter from Nesta or Norval. Cedella was prepared to miss her son in order to further his education, but when he dropped out of sight she began to suspect the father's motives in taking Nesta to Kingston.

Then one day a friend told her she had seen the boy on the street during a trip to the city. She traveled to the city herself, to the area where her friend reported him, and found Nesta living in the home of an elderly diabetic woman named Miss Gray. He was not attending school but acting as Miss Gray's errand boy. Cedella ignored the woman's protests and took her son out of Miss Gray's household and returned with him to his home in Nine Miles.

She wrote a furious letter to Norval but received no reply. His reasons for putting his son at the service of Miss Gray remain a mystery.

Cedella's relationship with Norval had been troubled from the beginning. On another trip to Kingston, she found he had married another woman and promptly took him to court on charges of bigamy. The aging Norval was acquitted when the court ruled him senile, and thus incompetent to bear responsibility for his actions. Nesta's relationship with his father was almost at an end anyway. Norval Marley died of a heart attack on May 20, 1955.

Nesta was later curious about his father. Was he a good man? Was he well-liked? What kind of life had he led? Cedella attempted to reassure the boy that his father was both good and well-respected, but she told him of the troubles they had as well.

Nesta did not seem to miss Kingston. He continued to play sports, did well in his studies, raced everywhere he went, and most importantly, continued to develop his musical talent. When he was about six or seven a cousin gave him his first musical instrument, a crude guitar made of goatskin and bamboo. He also met the boy who would later become a musical partner and band mate, Neville "Bunny" Livingston, whose father owned a small store in Nine Miles. The boys became inseparable, walking to school, playing sports and running through the bush together. Nesta developed an enduring love of the simple country lifestyle.

It was not easy, however, to make a living in Nine Miles. Cedella tried her hand at a variety of trades to feed herself and her family. She tried running a store, but when she allowed customers to buy items on credit people took advantage of her generosity and ran up bills they could never pay. She tried her hand as a "higgler," one of the vendors who sold fruit and vegetables on the street. Thieves stole her wares and she lost more than she sold.

Cedella was almost at wit's end when her brother John came to Nine Miles with a proposition. His wife was leaving their home in Kingston to study nursing. He invited Cedella to move to the city to keep house for him. She agreed, although it meant leaving Nesta behind with his grandfather Omeriah and his aunt Enid. Cedella thought she could make a better life for them if she left Nine Miles but constantly pined for her son during her early days in Kingston.

Another relative came through with yet another fortunate offer. Cedella's Aunt Ivy was living in a government subsidized home in Trench Town. Living with only her daughter for company, Aunt Ivy asked Cedella if she would like to move in. Cedella said she would move in if Nesta could join her. Ivy agreed and Nesta soon boarded a bus for the city.

In 1958, the thirteen-year-old arrived at his new home on Beckford Street in the Trench Town section of Kingston. His new neighborhood would teach Nesta some tough lessons in street life, and set his creative fires burning.

two
Wailers in Trench Town

Young Nesta Robert Marley went through a rough initiation during his early days in Trench Town. Other boys, sometimes in gangs, chased him and beat him up, and he suffered other abuse.

The main reason for the antagonism against Nesta was the color of his skin, which anyone not from Jamaica might find puzzling. More than 90 percent of the island's inhabitants were black or dark skinned, and would have been called "Negro" or "colored" in the United States of the 1950s. Many of the remainder were East Asian and Indian, and less than 1 percent of the population was European, or "white." The racial makeup was not simply black and white, but varied depending on slight differences of skin color. This color distinction was another bitter legacy of slavery.

Although Bob Marley never lived as a slave he had to suffer its consequences. Slavery had died a hard slow death and left in its wake a class system originally based on skin color.

Spaniards were the first people to exploit native Jamaicans as possessions. When Christopher Columbus landed in 1492 the natives of Jamaica were Arawaks, a people who had migrated from what is now Venezuela and Guyana around 700 BC. The Arawaks met the Spanish with gifts and feasts. Columbus wrote glowingly of the beautiful mountains and fields of the island nation.

The period of friendly relations did not last long. The Spanish colonized Jamaica in 1504, introducing bananas, citrus fruits, and sugarcane to grow there. They forced the Arawaks to work their plantations as serfs and massacred any who resisted. The Spanish also introduced new diseases, such

Christopher Columbus landed in Jamaica in 1492, leading the way for Spanish colonization of the island. *(Library of Congress)*

as smallpox and bubonic plague, which devastated the Arawak population. By 1598, the Arawak were almost extinct.

The Spanish turned to Africa for slaves to work the field. This forged a lasting link between Africa and Jamaica. Bob Marley's songs would often celebrate Africa as the spiritual home of him and other dark-skinned peoples.

In the 1600s, the Caribbean islands became a battleground for competing groups of European colonists. England invaded Jamaica in 1655 and dispelled the Spaniards. They continued the practice of kidnapping West Africans and forcing them to work on the sugar plantations. By the mid-1700s, sugar and slavery formed the backbone of a bustling outpost of the British empire, with around 430 plantations operating. British slavers used standard instruments of repression to keep their

A drawing of slaves working on a sugar plantation

slaves in line, including chains, branding irons and whipping posts. They would sometimes amputate limbs as punishment for escape attempts.

In the late seventeenth century the slaves in Jamaica staged a series of rebellions that would eventually earn their freedom. In 1690, in the parish of Clarendon, slaves escaped and fled to the mountains in the interior of the island, where they formed fighting bands. The British called them Maroons, a derogatory term derived from the Spanish term for escaped cattle, *cimarrones*. The Maroons used guerrilla warfare that eventually forced the British to free their slaves. Part of the island's musical heritage was forged in the battle against the invaders, as the rebel fighters used a hollow cow horn called an *abeng* to signal the arrival of British troops. The variations of tone conveyed different messages. The abeng helped the Maroons defeat better-armed and more numerous foes through musical communication.

The Maroons fought the English for almost fifty years, from 1690 to 1739, when the English settled by offering them freedom, hunting rights, and land. Fifty years of peace ensued, followed by the Second Maroon War, in which a group of rebel Maroons sided with a second wave of slave rebellions beginning in 1760. The brief rebellion ended with the British gaining the victory, aided by Maroons who helped track down their rebel counterparts.

But no victory built on the shaky foundation

An abeng

of the slave system could last forever. Resistance to slavery grew in the early 1800s among abolitionists in England. The slave trade was abolished in 1808, leaving the plantations dependent on those born into slavery. Further slave rebellions finally convinced the British they could not continue the economy they had built on the backs of African servants. In 1838, the British abolished slavery in Jamaica.

An insidious remnant of the institution remained in the class system that began in the wake of abolition. Some slave women had become pregnant from their masters and these lighter-skinned descendants were called mulattoes. In many cases, their white fathers gave them access to the same privileges enjoyed by whites, including entry to trades, professions, and military rank. When a system of voting rights was introduced based on property, the mulattoes ascended in the social order by virtue of owning land. Black resistance against mulattoes and whites boiled over in the Morant Bay Rebellion of 1865. Former slaves killed dozens of police and plantation owners. In turn, the British executed hundreds of the rioters. They also abolished parliament and declared Jamaica a crown colony, under the direct rule of the British throne. This government survived well into the twentieth century, until Jamaica was declared an independent country in 1962.

The long struggle over race left Jamaicans intensely sensitive on the issue of color. Nesta's problems stemmed from having a white father. The bullies who tormented him saw different hues. From one beating to the next, he might be singled out for being white, yellow, brown, or red.

Once he attempted to make a girlfriend, only to be rejected by the girl's family for being white. He questioned his mother why he had to endure such cruelty.

"Why am I this person?" he asked. "Why is my father white and not black like everybody else? What did I do wrong?" Cedella did not have an answer.

An ally soon arrived. Nesta's friend "Bunny" came from Nine Miles, accompanied by his father Thaddeus. Thaddeus, or "Mr. Taddy" as he was known, began a relationship with Cedella. Mr. Taddy was sometimes abusive to Nesta's mother, but he was the closest to a father the boy had in Kingston.

Music became a refuge for Nesta and Bunny. They bought radios and listened to stations in Miami and New Orleans, forming the foundation of their musical education on American artists. Throughout the 1950s, they listened to rockers such as Ricky Nelson, Fats Domino, and Elvis Presley. They also heard rhythm and blues, including songs by Ray Charles and Lloyd Price, and became fans of American singing groups, such as the Impressions and the Drifters.

Nesta began to yearn to become a musician. He dropped out of school, while Bunny continued his education. He later said his lack of interest in formal education was a result of a curriculum that emphasized European accomplishments above all other cultures, including those of his dark skinned ancestors. "What about the tradition of the African people?" he later said. "We want to learn that in school. We don't want to learn about Christopher Columbus and all of that."

The strongest influence school would leave on Nesta and Bunny was a strong love of team sports. Both played soccer and cricket. Nesta would continue to play soccer whenever he could, even as a grown man. He considered sports a great way to clear his mind.

Nesta grew more determined to make a living as a musician, but Cedella was afraid music might not provide a stable income. She urged him to learn a trade and at her insistence he took a job welding. Nesta did not much care for welding, but he made a valuable friend in the welding yards. Desmond Dekker also loved music and the two would sing together, and even wrote some songs.

One day Desmond went to a small recording company called Beverley's, run by Jamaicans of Chinese origin. Beverley's had started as a record store and its owners had branched into recording and selling original Jamaican music. Desmond made a record with Beverley's called "Honour Your Mother and Father" that became a local hit. Desmond did not make much money from his record, but he did gain a lot of pride. Nesta was awed by his friend's accomplishment.

Desmond and Nesta quit the welding yard after each suffered an eye injury. Nesta did not fret at the loss of his welding job. He only wanted to sing and write his own music. He began associating almost solely with musicians.

His peers among the aspiring musicians helped him shake free of his childhood name. They called him Robert or Bob, not Nesta.

His homeland offered young Bob Marley inspiration. The streets of Kingston echoed with a raucous mix of musical styles during the 1950s and '60s. Jazz was making its influence felt everywhere, including Jamaica. Jazz is a form of music known for its syncopation, elaborate improvisation, and blending of diverse melodies. Calypso was the island's most distinctive music, combining American jazz with improvised lyrics that often satirized local people and events. Jamaican bands also began to play rhythm and blues, a mix of African American blues and folk music.

Another musical form began to emerge as bands continued to search out a sound that would set them apart. They mixed horns and guitars with rhythm and blues and jazz and came up with a sound called "ska," a name derived from the distinctive sound of the guitars, which sounded like the sound *scat* to some listeners.

The sound in the street and at parties did not much resemble the tunes heard on the radio. Most stations played only pop and rock from the United States, reflecting an infatuation with all things American. A group of Jamaican musicians and deejays decided to offer an alternative to the radio fare. They did not own radio stations, so they outfitted trucks with speakers and megaphones and played their music in the streets. They played at lawn parties, with rival deejays setting up on opposite sides to compete. Deejays arrived dressed in outrageous costumes, donning capes and masks for the night's entertainment. They began talking over the music, making cynical wisecracks about one another, the musicians, even audience members. Such patter was called "toasting" and is similar to the methods of the early rappers in the U.S.

One of the best known street deejays was Coxsone Dodd, who referred to himself as "Sir Coxsone." Born in 1932 in Kingston, Dodd traveled to the United States as a young man seeking work. He found the work he sought on Florida farms, and also discovered a passion for American music. He traveled to record stores in New York and Chicago in search of rhythm and blues, and jazz. He sent the records home to his mother, who played them in her grocery store to attract customers. He had plenty of music to play when the war of the party deejays began.

Coxsone Dodd, a popular street deejay, had a recording studio inside Coxsone's Music City record store. *(Courtesy of Redfern Music Picture Library)*

Dodd and his rivals searched out American records and scratched the names off the labels to make it harder for others to find out the names of songs. Dodd's style of toasting was nasty and personal. His speakers, huge for the time, all carried Dodd's name." When rap became popular years later, Dodd claimed to have invented it.

Dodd got into the recording business almost as an afterthought. He started recording local artists at Federal Studios in Kingston. He initially wanted the recordings to enliven his sound system shows but the local musicians proved so popular with the crowds that he opened Coxsone's Music

City record store. Music City became one of Bob Marley's favorite hangouts.

Desmond Dekker, Bob's old friend from the welding yard, encouraged him to write some songs for Dodd. In early 1962, Bob showed up at Federal Studios with three of his compositions, hoping to meet Dodd and perform for him. Instead, he was met by Leslie Kong, who also produced records at Federal. Kong listened to Bob's music and immediately signed him to a contract. Kong put out a single with the song "Judge Not" as the "A" side or top single. "Judge Not" came from Jesus' exhortation to his followers, "Judge not, lest you be judged," one of grandfather Omeriah's favorite Bible verses. On the flip side was a tune called "Do You Still Love Me?" Bob was paid twenty pounds, about forty U.S. dollars, and two acetate copies, for the session.

Neither song became a hit, but the Federal recording launched Bob's career. He was not concerned with immediate fame or success; he just wanted his music to be heard. It filled him with pride to hear "Judge Not" ringing out from the same jukebox speakers from which he had first heard his musical idols. He followed up his debut record with two more songs, "One Cup of Coffee" and "Terror."

Bob's solo career with Kong did not last long. The producer failed to pay him for the later songs, and Bob quit dealing with him. The experience had increased his musical confidence, however, and he continued his search for a more reliable producer.

Bob wanted to be part of a group. It was in his nature to enjoy singing with other people. He also felt he would have more leverage with producers, both in terms of pay and artistic freedom, if he had other artists on his side. The first person he sought out, naturally, was Bunny. His old friend was initially reluctant. Bunny was getting good grades in school and had even made plans to attend Howard University in Washington, D.C. Now Bob wanted him to risk everything for the uncertainty of a musical career.

Bob used every tactic he could think of to wear down Bunny's resistance, including making him feel guilty. Bob told Bunny it was he who had gotten him involved in making music to begin with, stretching the truth considerably. But it worked. "He just kept on keeping on like that until I decided, okay, what else am I going to do?" Bunny said later.

The two then set about making up a name for the band. They initially saw themselves following in the path of American rock, and rhythm and blues bands, such as the Platters, the Drifters, and Frankie Lymon and the Teenagers. They decided to call themselves the Teenagers, then changed their minds as they realized they would seem like copycats. They then decided on the Wailin' Wailers, before shorting it to simply the Wailers. Bunny eventually dropped the last name Livingston and began calling himself Bunny Wailer. To the two founding members, the Wailers evoked protest. Trench Town was full of people who suffered from poverty and violence. The Wailers wanted to cry out for them. The band's name was a symbol of their mission.

Bunny recruited an angry young man from West Road who fit in perfectly with the image he and Bob wanted. Peter Tosh had been born in 1944 as Winston Hubert McIntosh. He had been raised by his aunt. Six feet and five inches tall, Peter was a rugged man who loved outdoor sports, martial arts, and music. When he was a child, family members took him to church almost every time the doors were open, but

An early photograph of the original Wailers: Bunny Livingston (left), Bob Marley (middle), and Peter Tosh (right). *(Courtesy of Getty Images/Michael Ochs Archives)*

dragging him there became more of a task as he grew older. Peter hated how the Christian religion was taught. He questioned why all the prophets, including Jesus, were portrayed as blue-eyed white men. The desperate lives people lived in Trench Town also embittered him and came to blame authority for social ills. He began renaming the parts of the world around him. He called "Kingston" by the name of "Killsome," decried the "system" as the "sh-tseme." "Oppressors" became "downpressors." Peter Tosh came into the Wailers with a philosophy of his own and a rage that fit well with the image the band sought.

The three began practicing at the home of Joe Higgs, a musician who lived not far from Bob. Higgs had made a hit record of his own in 1960, "Manny-O," by the Higgs and Wilson duet. He became a mentor to the Wailers. Singing in Higgs' yard, the Wailers picked up three more members. Junior Braithwhite joined the band, as did two female singers, Beverly Kelso and Cherry Green. Bob asked Kelso to join after hearing her sing in a teen club. Higgs recruited Green after hearing her sing in her yard. This lineup was the Wailers that Jamaicans heard in their early years.

In December of 1963, when Bob was eighteen, a musician friend finally introduced the Wailers to Coxsone Dodd. By then Dodd had become quite successful as a producer. He operated five record labels, as well as the recording studio, Jamaica Recording and Publishing, Studio One. When they entered the audition room, the Wailers found Dodd sitting on a high stool at the end of the room, frowning at the new arrivals. It was Dodd's nature to intimidate those who would work for him.

Dodd listened to the Wailers and made sure they understood he was not immediately convinced. They played several songs before Peter suggested they perform a song Bob had written a couple of years before called "Simmer Down."

"Simmer Down" was a message song aimed at the gangs of young Jamaicans called "Rude Boys." Rude Boys were rebels, their anger driven by the poverty and class divisions of Jamaica, but had no philosophy other than violence and crime. In the early to mid-1960s, the Rude Boys clashed with police, developing a reputation as thugs. The Wailers were from the same background as the Rude Boys and understood their anger. Bob had earned his street name "Tuff Gong" by scrapping with such guys, fighting frequently to live down his mixed parentage. But "Simmer Down," as its title suggests, was a call for the Rude Boys to control their tempers. The Wailers were the perfect messengers for the warning because the gangs were some of their biggest fans.

The Wailers had used the song as a warm-up number and Bob had wanted to rewrite it but had not yet done so. He and the other Wailers had already observed its soothing effect on its target audience. When the band played "Simmer Down," the Rude Boys did not fight. They danced.

Coxsone Dodd was delighted by the song. After hearing it, he offered to sign them. He would act as the band's manager and producer. The terms of the Wailers' contract, however, were not generous. Dodd would pay them only twenty pounds per song.

Dodd wanted to release "Simmer Down" as a single. The night after they sang it for their first recording session, the Wailers went to a dance party where Dodd's speakers were set up. They were amazed to find that Dodd was already playing the song. Their rise to fame came almost as fast. By February of 1964, "Simmer Down" had sold 70,000 copies, earning it the number one spot on the Jamaican charts.

The Wailers were not the only hit group on the island, but they had cut their own niche. People began to shout "Wailer!" when they saw any of the members on the street. Fame brought its own rewards, of course, but there was something the fans did not know. Most assumed the Wailers were rich as well as famous and Dodd helped them keep up their image by outfitting them in sharp suits and dresses. But he pocketed almost all of their profits, doling out only meager salaries. At a time when their music was being played all over the island, the Wailers were so poor they had to share a single flour and sugar cake for lunch; each band member was allowed one bite. They had more in common with their poor fans than the fans realized.

Later in his career, after his musical style evolved from pop to reggae, Bob had little good to say about his early producers. "In de beginnin', every people rob and cheat you," he said. "Dem was some bad pirates, mon, comin' down like Dracula on reggae."

The Rude Boys continued to loyally follow the Wailers, sometimes creating a raucous atmosphere at concerts. During one performance the electricity went out in the hall and onstage. The Wailers found themselves with dead amps, surrounded by angry fans and a chorus of boos. Instinctively, their Rude Boy fans assumed it was part of some plot to stop the show and hurled bottles at the stage. The Wailers locked themselves in a bathroom until police got the riot under control. They later found out the cause of the power failure was no conspiracy, but an islandwide blackout.

As he was first becoming famous, Bob was confronted by a new kind of loneliness. His mother opened the mail one day to find an invitation from her Aunt Ivy to join her in Delaware. Cedella quickly agreed to move. Making a living in Jamaica was difficult and she believed the United States would offer her more opportunity.

Cedella found the United States to be as prosperous as she had imagined it. She was astonished at ordinary grocery stores, where such simple items as eggs and bread could be had cheaply. "Here, stretched out as far as the eye could see, were opportunity and prosperity," she wrote later. "I buckled down to work hard for my share." She soon had a housekeeping job paying forty dollars a week, a royal sum by her previous standards. But for Bob, a much valued family link was reduced to letters and the occasional phone call.

A fortunate coincidence helped ease the pain of separation from his mother. As Bob and the Wailers made their way to Studio One each day, they began to encounter a young girl who would change Bob's life and make her own contribution to the group. Her name was Alpharita Constantia Anderson, but friends called her Rita.

Rita was a nursing student, but her real love was music. She sang with her two friends Constantine "Dream" Walker and Marlene "Precious" Gifford. Rita knew the Wailers passed her house on their way to the studio and was determined to meet them. Peter Tosh was the first to speak to her. The next time they saw him, the three sang him the song "What's Your Name?" by the American duo Sam and Dave.

Peter liked what he heard and suggested they go to Dodd's studio and try out. Dodd also liked the trio and offered them one of his standard contracts. He thought they sounded a lot like the soul group The Marvelettes, and so Rita, Dream, and Precious became the Soulettes.

The Soulettes backed up the Wailers and other groups in Dodd's stable of artists. Rita was immediately attracted to Bob. "He was pretty handsome . . . I looked at him and thought, uh-oh, such a *nice* guy. And I got weak in the knees." After going on a movie date, Rita and Bob began a steady relationship.

Rita saw not only musical talent in the Wailers but ambition. They wanted to be as big as any of the American bands they heard on the radio and worked hard to accomplish their dream. They arrived on time for recording sessions and remained focused until a song was finished. But Dodd often treated the Wailers as a mere tool to further his own ambitions. He made them record music that had nothing to do with their own mission as a band, such as covers of pop hits like "What's New, Pussycat?" and "White Christmas."

The Wailers recorded more than a hundred songs for Dodd without receiving more than a minuscule fraction of the profits. His stinginess with the band would take a toll. The year 1966 was a hard one for the Wailers. They would lose three original members—and one of them was Bob Marley.

three
Rastaman

Sometimes it seemed to the Wailers that Bob Marley was a tyrant in the studio. He would stop a song in the middle because of a bad note and angrily turn on the offending musician. His anger could reduce Beverly Kelso to tears. Later he would try to console her. "Oh, Beverly, you know how I am." She did understand; Bob was a perfection-ist about the music.

Another of Bob's habits was not so easy for her to accept. He, along with all the other Wailers, smoked marijuana at the studio. They did not just smoke after work but all the time, including recording sessions. Studio One was almost airtight and the air filled with smoke. The band would laugh at jokes that made no sense to anyone who was not stoned, and she felt left out.

The Wailers' use of marijuana came about, at least in part, from exposure to Rastafari or Rasta, a religion born in Jamaica. Their mentor Joe Higgs was a follower, having

Some of the tenets of the Rastafari faith include growing hair into dreadlocks, abiding by an *ital* diet, and smoking ganja. *(Courtesy of AP Images/Boris Heger)*

become one well before recording his first Jamaican hit single. He taught the kids who practiced in his yards the tenets of the Rastafari faith, such as wearing of long, uncombed hair knotted in dreadlocks, and the *ital* diet, which discourages the eating of shellfish and pork, as well as the use of alcohol. Rastas preferred vegetables and fruits, including the coconuts and mangoes found in tropical climates. They also used ganja or marijuana, both as an ingredient in food and in smoked form. Rastas consider ganja a sacred herb, with prayers devoted to its consumption.

The two people most revered by Rastas were Marcus Garvey, a Jamaican who advocated a pro-Africa movement, and Haile Selassie I, emperor of the African nation of Ethiopia. Bob Marley would come to revere Garvey and worship Selassie. He sang of the emperor and used his photos on album covers.

Garvey prepared the way for Selassie's rise as a sacred figure among the Rastas. Garvey was born on August 17, 1887,

Marcus Garvey championed the pro-Africa Rastafarian movement. *(Library of Congress)*

in the town of St. Ann's Bay. He worked in the printing business in Kingston, moved to London for a university education, then to New York, where he became a street speaker. He was an electrifying orator and a flamboyant leader. He sometimes wore green and purple robes through the African American section of Harlem. He outraged U.S. black leaders of the time, who were calling for integration of the races, by preaching that the black races should unite and return to Africa. Only there, Garvey said, could people of African descent establish their own nation and rid themselves of the vestiges of slavery. In 1922, Garvey met with leaders of the Ku Klux Klan in Georgia and declared the Klansmen honest Americans for admitting they wanted a whites-only country. Such actions destroyed his credibility in the American civil rights movements. In 1927, the government ended Garvey's career as a black leader in the United States when it indicted him for mail fraud. Garvey was deported and returned to Jamaica.

He continued for the rest of his life to advocate a return to Africa for all those who had ancestors on the continent. "Look to Africa for the crowning of a Black King," Garvey said, "He shall be the Redeemer."

When Ras Tafari Makonnen was crowned emperor of Ethiopia in 1930, taking the name Haile Selassie I, some Jamaicans saw him as the fulfillment of both Garvey's prediction and prophecy in the Bible. (*Ras* means "prince"; Tafari was the emperor's given name). A line in Psalms reads "Princes shall come out of Egpyt; Ethiopia shall stretch out her hands to God." Selassie was also called King of Kings, Lord of Lords, Root of David and other Biblical names by his subjects, lending weight to the Rastas' belief that he was anointed by God.

The Rastafari faith is not an organized religion and followers interpret it differently. Its interpretation of both the Bible and Selassie's words are highly subjective, varying according to believers. Selassie never made any claim to lead the Rastas, nor was he a Rasta himself. He was a member of the Ethiopian Orthodox Church, an affiliation expected of an Ethiopian emperor. Yet the Rastafari movement continued to grow after his death in 1975. Some Rastas claim

Haile Selassie I *(Library of Congress)*

Selassie's death was a hoax and the emperor is still alive.

The Rastas made their own contributions to the mix of English and African-derived words that make up the Jamaican patois, the island's colorful manner of speaking. Rasta had deliberately attacked and remolded English as a symbolic protest against the empire which had enslaved their ancestors. They often changed words based on the way they sounded. "Dedicate" sounded like it began with "dead" to Rasta ears; they substituted *liv-icate*. Likewise, they dismantled "participate" on the grounds that it sounded like only "part" of those called would take part in a venture. *Full-ticipate* sounded better to their ears.

They also coined original words. A Rasta discussion of spiritual matters is called a *reasoning.* A celebration or holiday is a *grounation. Livity* is the natural lifestyle based on the ital diet, while *irie* refers to something judged to be joyous, positive, cool. The Rasta allowed their hair to grow into long uncombed braids. Their appearance was frightening to more conventional Jamaicans, and the Rasta word dreadlocks refers to the fear caused by their ropy locks. They did not call their sacramental drug marijuana, but ganja.

Beverly found herself standing against a powerful system of beliefs when she objected to the Wailers smoking ganja. When she complained, the other band members told her she should start smoking but she refused. Beverly stewed resentment as the Wailers continued to smoke while recording.

The poor money they were making added to the pressures. Cherry Green, who was supporting a child, grew tired of performing in poverty and was the first of the original six to quit the group. Beverly quit soon after, despite the other members' pleas for her to stay.

The terrible pay was wearing on Bob as well. Since his mother's departure he had been almost homeless, sleeping in a spare room at Studio One. His mother Cedella had been urging him to come live with her in Delaware. Early in 1966, he wrote a letter taking her up on the offer.

He did not intend to live the rest of his life in the United States. He wanted only enough money to start his own record label in Jamaica. But before he left, he wanted to take the next step in his relationship with Rita. On February 10, 1966, the two were married. He left for the United States two days later.

Bob arrived in Philadelphia on a cold winter's night. He was met by Cedella and her new husband Edward Booker.

Booker worked at a car dealership and made a good living. The reunion was joyous, with everyone laughing as they rode back to the Booker house in Delaware. After going without a real home for so long, Bob considered his mother's house practically a mansion. He could not believe the size of his room.

But he needed to make and save money to make his trip to the United States worthwhile. He first tried to get a job as a stevedore, one of the dock workers who load and unload ships. His stepfather was dubious about Bob's chances, because being a stevedore was a physically hard job and the young man had a slight build. Cedella tried to help him by dressing him in layers of shirts and sweaters, with big boots so he would look larger than he was. But the crew's boss saw through the disguise and told Bob he was not big enough to do the lifting the job required.

Bob finally got a job as a janitor at the Dupont Hotel. During his off-time, he practiced his guitar and wrote songs. For a while, he remained low key about his Rasta beliefs. He even consented to get his hair cut for his job search, a practice prohibited by most Rastas. He could only go so far, however, in compromising his beliefs.

One day he came upon his mother preparing breakfast, cooking bacon in a pan. "Is a dangerous something dat, you know, Mamma." Cedella demanded to know how bacon was dangerous.

"It come from de swine where Jesus cast de devil," Bob replied. "Is a unclean animal." Afterwards she prepared toast, jam and porridge for his breakfasts.

Bob was not strident about his beliefs, but he did try to convert his mother, telling Cedella she was already a Rasta

whether she knew it or not. He was sure in time she would come to accept Haile Selassie as God. He would occasionally go with her to church, but made clear he did not accept her religion as his own.

One afternoon Cedella came home from work with a load of groceries. While Bob helped her unload them, he told her he had a vision while he slept on the couch. He dreamed that a man in a felt cap and embroidered coat had entered the room and taken a ring from his pocket. He placed the ring on Bob's finger. Cedella told him he must have had a dream of his father. The Captain had wanted to give Bob the dream ring, she said, because he had been able to give him so little in life.

She gave Bob a ring of her husband's to wear in its place. But he did not think it felt right, and gave it back to her. He later told her he had come to a different interpretation of the dream.

"Dat wasn't me father, Mamma," he said. "Dat was His Majesty Haile Selassie I."

With most people, Bob was far less insistent about preaching the Rasta beliefs. When he advanced in his temporary career by getting a job at the Newark Chrysler plant, he showed his faith by wearing the Rasta colors of red, gold, and green on a brimless hat.

He spoke little about Rasta or music with other workers. He told other employees that he had a band, but not much more. He kept a diary, including lyrics to songs he had written, but showed it to no one. Most of his coworkers assumed he was just one more guy working to pay his bills. Bob may have been tight-lipped but he was not unfriendly. Other Chrysler workers remember him for his musical Jamaican lilt, talking

to other employees about music while playing dominoes during his breaks.

Bob did make one close friend during his time in Delaware. Ibis Pitts ran a gift shop in Wilmington, where he sold African clothing and jewelry. Pitts was also a musician. He began coming over to Bob's house, where the two would jam in Bob's basement. Pitts would play the conga drums while Bob played guitar and sang. Although he thought the Wailers were superior to much of the slick pop music of the time, Bob liked some American and British bands. He listened to the Beatles' "Eleanor Rigby," a song about a woman who leads a futile and dreary existence, over and over. The last stanza tells of the title character's lonely death: "Eleanor Rigby died in the church and was buried along with her name." What Bob heard in the song is anyone's guess, but there is no doubt he wanted his life to count for more than Eleanor Rigby's had.

Bob would later paint his experience in the United States as an exposure to a culture driven to frenzy by the drive for money and material goods. "Everything too fast, too noisy, too rush-rush in Delaware," he complained to his mother.

He considered his manual labor jobs a dead end. He did not like anything that got in the way of his creativity or freedom. He even began to question whether his marriage to Rita was too much of a restraint.

When he first arrived in Delaware, he had told his mother that he was married. He placed wedding pictures on her mantle. Months later, having had no contact with his wife except by letters, he began to deny having gone through the ceremony of his own free will. He claimed he had been coerced into marrying Rita and expressed cynicism about the institution of marriage. It may seem odd for Bob to have felt the first stirrings of discontent about his vows to Rita during a time they were thousands of miles apart, but it signaled the beginning of stormy years in their relationship. As late as the late 1970s, Bob would tell interviewers he was not married. His mother Cedella faithfully took her son's side, however, and believed his tale that he had somehow been tricked into marriage.

When Rita flew to Delaware in August of 1966 the Marley family downplayed any rift between the two. Cedella charmed Rita with tales of her childhood in St. Ann, and Rita helped Bob catch up on news from Jamaica. Things were much the same between the Wailers and Coxsone Dodd. The band had continued to play without Bob and the producer was still paying them peanuts. Bunny was hoping the band could hold together long enough for Bob to rejoin them.

Rita had witnessed an event Bob sorely regretted having missed, a visit to Jamaica by Haile Selassie I. More than 100,000 people had turned out to greet the emperor when his plane touched down at the airport. It had been a rainy morning with lightning streaking from the clouds, but soon after the emperor's plane landed, the sun broke out. The sunshine arriving with Haile Selassie's plane was only one of many portentous events that day.

Rita had fixed her hair and put on her best dress in hopes of joining the welcoming crowd, but the throngs of admirers were so thick she never made it to the airport. People near her began shouting as the motorcade got closer. She expected someone of imposing stature, in proportion to the esteem in which he was held by the Rastas, but saw instead a short man wearing an officer's cap and a khaki uniform decked out in medals. Rastas who recorded or worked at Studio One had told her that Selassie would have stigmata, or wounds resembling Christ's crucifixion scars, in his palms. When the emperor lifted his hands to the adoring crowd, Rita said, she indeed saw the scars. The emperor's eyes locked on hers and she felt herself linked with divinity in that moment. Her encounter with the emperor was the defining point in Rita's embrace of the Ratafari religion.

Had he been in Jamaica, nothing would have stopped Bob from seeing Emperor Selassie's visit. Hearing Rita describe her mystical brush with the Rastas' iconic leader must have only added to his longing to return home. He had come to the United States in search of money. By the time of Rita's visit, he had accumulated a nest egg. It was not as much as he had hoped, but it would go further in Jamaica than in the States. He was still bent on recording his own songs, without Coxsone Dodd's hand in his back pocket.

Not long after Rita's visit, the Chrysler plant laid Bob off. He applied for unemployment compensation, but would have little time to collect it. In October, he got a notice from the Selective Service Board ordering him to register for the draft. At the time, the United States was fighting the Vietnam War and there was no way Bob Marley was going to become Private Marley in the service of the U.S. Army. He packed his things and caught a flight to Kingston. One of the few keepsakes of his time in the States that he carried home was the ring his mother had given him, because she insisted it was a sign from God.

four

Cold Journey

When Bob landed in Kingston in the fall of 1966, he carried a notebook packed with the songs he had written in Delaware. Other musicians on the island had also kept creating new material. The music scene in Jamaica was churning out new bands with a variety of new sounds.

The hottest thing going was "rock steady," which had evolved out of ska. The horns were less prominent in rock steady and it emphasized vocal and guitar solos, fueled by a powerful bass. Bob tweaked some of his songs into a rock steady style, and wrote some new songs in the style as well. Some artists fade when faced with change, but Jamaica's musical evolution inspired Bob.

He returned to a Studio One that Coxsone Dodd had transformed with techniques and equipment he had bought from England. The studio could now isolate instrumental and vocal breaks, refining them to perfection before laying them

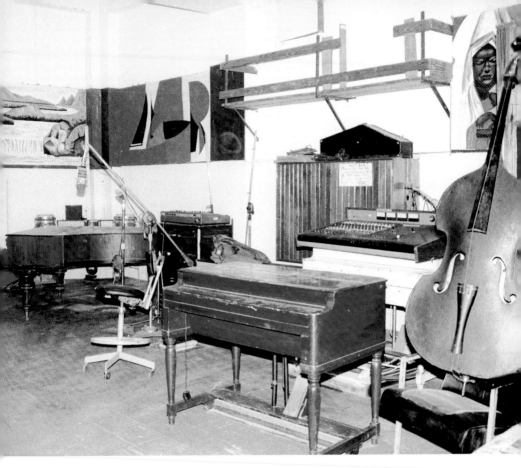

When Bob returned to Jamaica from America, he discovered Dodd had made improvements to Studio One, pictured here. *(Courtesy of UrbanImage. tv/Ron Veste)*

into the tracks. This was not uncommon in Britain and the United States, but marked a great step forward for Dodd.

Bob took his notebook out during his first session back at Studio One and propped it on a stool. He played his guitar and sang his new songs as the Wailers listened, then joined in, almost effortlessly merging into a rock steady style. Some of the songs were love songs, not much different than the music Bob had written before. Others bore the influence of his time in the U.S., such as "It's Alright," a tune about keeping one's individuality while working a monotonous job. Bob could write lyrics that touched on inner anger, yet sing in a way that seemed sweet and vulnerable. Coxsone Dodd had little tenderness in him, but he instantly recognized the power of such a mix. After listening to the songs, Dodd told Bob he was already ahead of the rock steady pack.

Even so, Bob wanted to get out of Dodd's grasp. The producer had spent plenty on equipment, but his rates to musicians had not improved. Bob had come home with seven hundred U.S. dollars. That would last for a while in Jamaica in the 1960s, but it was not enough to set up an independent studio. He had to compromise and decided to open a store selling Dodd's records at Rita's aunt's house on Greenwich Park Road. The profits, along with his savings, allowed him to start his own label, Wail 'N' Soul 'M, named after its first two bands, the Wailers and Rita's Soulettes.

Wail 'N' Soul 'M's first release featured Bob's song "Bend Down Low," with blues style lyrics chiding a former lover

One of Bob Marley's notebooks with set lists and lyrics written in Marley's handwriting (*Courtesy of AP Images/Jason DeCrow*)

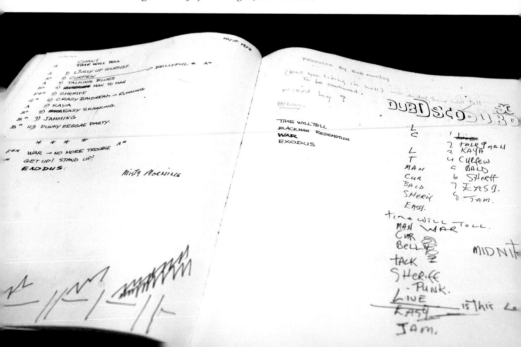

for "livin' in sin." The B side featured Bob and Rita singing a song reaffirming their love, titled "Hold on to This Feeling." During the short time he ran his own label, Bob was always strapped for the money it took to distribute the records. He delivered his own records to the stores on his bike. He ran out of money and had to shut down Wail 'N' Soul 'M after a year, reluctantly returning to Studio One.

Bob and Rita moved out of Kingston, to a farm at Nine Miles. Despite their poverty it was one of the happiest times of their marriage. They grew yams, cabbage, and potatoes, living and eating simply. They got a pet donkey named Nimble that followed Bob wherever he went, eating out of his hand. Bob strummed his guitar and wrote songs away from the hustle and bustle of the studio and the city.

The Wailers' dealings with Dodd grew ever more strained. The breaking point came one afternoon when Bob was not present. Dodd asked Peter Tosh to accompany another artist on keyboards. This was a common request at studios but Tosh exploded. A shouting match broke out, with the other Wailers taking Peter's side. Someone called the police, and Bunny began hurling insults at them as well.

So began a series of clashes between the band and the Kingston police. It may have been the incident at the studio, or the band's use of the illegal herb marijuana, but the Wailers seemed to have been marked by the authorities. The police busted Bunny and two other Trench Town musicians for ganja on a street corner in 1967. Bunny had no pot in his possession, but when the case went to trial, he was the only one convicted. He served a year and two months in prison. Bob was arrested for a minor traffic offense and spent forty-eight hours in jail. The word on the street was that the police wanted to put the whole band behind bars.

With their bad reputation growing, and ties broken with Dodd, the Wailers were reduced to recording for Leslie Kong, the producer who had reneged on payment for some of Bob's early tunes. Kong produced a handful of records with the Wailers before they teamed up with a producer who identified with their problems all too well.

Lee "Scratch" Perry would turn out to be the best and most creative of the Wailers' Jamaican producers. He had an ear and feel for the band far beyond the grasp of Leslie Kong or Coxsone Dodd. Most importantly, he would help guide the Wailers as they transformed into one of the world's first reggae bands.

Perry, who had also started as an artist with Studio One, was a hard-drinking and hot-tempered man who founded a band called The Upsetters. They released the songs "Run for Cover" and "The Upsetter," both of which climbed to the top of the Jamaican charts. In 1969, The Upsetters released "Return of Django." Toots Hibbart and the Maytalls had released a song called "Do the Reggay" in 1968 and would go on to cut some of the early reggae tunes, but the Upsetters' songs made a greater stir.

Reggae used the electric bass, often at a high volume, as the lead instrument. Organ, piano and drums added to build a richness of sound. Melodies tended to be short and constantly repeated. Most importantly, reggae lyrics were about class division and social injustice. As reggae evolved, it most frequently represented the Rasta lifestyle, with references to ganja, dreadlocks, and the spiritual life.

Bob's relationship with "Scratch" Perry began with an angry feud. Perry had taken the Upsetters to England, hoping to capitalize on the success of "Return of Django," and introduce British youth to the new sound. They were a colossal hit, but as usual, most of their money went to the producers.

Bob was astonished that a Jamaican band could rouse such enthusiasm from British audiences. The Upsetters were astonished that they could create such a sensation without making more money. They began grousing with the Wailers and, soon enough, jamming with them. Bob took things a step farther when he asked them to join the Wailers for recording sessions, including "Man to Man," "Duppy Conquerer," and "Soul Almighty," as well as songs from his Delaware note-book. Bob set the stage for a huge confrontation when he approached the Upsetters about quitting Perry's band and join-ing the Wailers, and the Upsetters unanimously agreed.

Bob's theft of his very successful band enraged Perry and he threatened to kill Bob. Amid rumors of bloodshed, the two musicians held a face to face meeting. Tempers eventu-ally cooled, and they struck a compromise. The two decided Perry would be the Wailers' exclusive producer. During the meeting to settle the rift, Bob and Scratch even collaborated on a song. It was called "Small Axe," a symbolic threat to the big producers who were robbing the musicians. It referred to the Jamaican folk saying that a small ax could topple a big tree.

Bob and Rita continued to refine their Rasta beliefs, attending sacred ceremonies and talking to teachers of the faith. Mortimo Planno of the Divine Theocratic Temple of Rastafari in Kingston became one of Bob's mentors. He told Planno of his dream in Delaware, when the man entered the room and placed a ring on his finger. Planno's interpreta-tion was not quite so cheerful as Cedella's, who had said

Bob Marley convinced The Upsetters (*above*) to leave Lee Perry and join the Wailers. (*Courtesy of Getty Images/Michael Ochs Archives*)

the man must have been Bob's late father trying to make amends. Planno said the dream could have two meanings: either he would grow in his Rasta faith or "ketch a fire," meaning catch Hell.

Planno introduced Bob to Johnny Nash, an American musician who had played on the popular Arthur Godfrey *Talent Scouts* program and made a hit in the United States with his 1958 song "A Very Special Love." Nash had been born in Houston, Texas in 1940 and had been a choirboy before being discovered by Godfrey at the age of thirteen. At the time he met Bob, Nash was basking in the success of his recent single "Hold Me Tight." Bob played several of his songs for Nash and his manager, Danny Sims. Sims quickly offered Bob and the Wailers a songwriting contract with his company Cayman Music. But Sims gave Bob a piece of advice that might have changed reggae history for the worse if Bob had taken it to heart.

"Him se me voice not good enough, but me songs are," Bob said. Sims urged Bob to concentrate on songwriting, and forget singing.

Throughout the late 1960s and early '70s, Bob Marley and the Wailers made records for both Sims and Perry. Unlike Sims, Perry saw great potential in Bob's voice. The former front man for the Upsetters drilled the Wailers into fine form, coaching Bob to drop a falsetto he had used in early songs in favor of a clearer, stronger vocal line. He made a deal with Trojan records to cut the Wailers first album *Soul Rebels*. The album featured songs that had already reached the top of Jamaican charts but had not been introduced to wider audiences. Although it did not get much airplay, *Soul Rebels* sold well to the "roots" audience that formed the core of Wailers fans.

Sims failed to use the Wailers to their full potential. At times, his decisions were worse than Dodd's, such as when he had them record a weird novelty record called "Milk Shake and Potato Chips," about a girl who ignores her fiancé for the sake of junk food. This was a far cry from the music that had energized the Rude Boy dance halls.

The American producer made up for some of his bad decisions when he got Bob signed with the CBS International recording company, even while keeping him under contract with his songwriting company. Sims also offered Bob the chance to record some songs for the upcoming Johnny Nash movie *Want So Much to Believe*. In 1971, Bob flew to Stockholm, Sweden to work on the soundtrack.

Peter (from left), Bunny, Rita, and Bob perform at Johnny Nash's house in Kingston, Jamaica. Bob's manager, Danny Simms, stands behind them with a microphone. *(Courtesy of UrbanImage.tv/Trax/Astley Chin)*

The trip brought mixed blessings. Bob hated the cold of northern Europe but loved the Scandinavian cities. He lived in the studio basement, working on songs for long hours during the time he was not recording. Sims had wanted to add some Jamaican "spice" to the movie soundtrack, and Bob was happy to oblige, taking joy in teaching reggae licks to other musicians. On the other hand, he hated the pork dishes frequently served at meals and would slink back to his basement room to avoid the smell.

He became fast friends with John "Rabbit" Bundrick, who later became famous as a keyboard player for the rock band the Who. Bundrick remembered the experience fondly. "We were all just very creative musicians, singers and song-writers, living together in the same house, working on the same projects," he said. "We had so much fun together, just a party for twenty-four hours a day."

None of Bob's songs made it to the movie soundtrack, which turned out just as well, since the film flopped. But Sims did arrange for the Wailers to do a British tour. The tour was less than satisfactory, with the Wailers spending most of their time playing assembly halls in British secondary schools, along with a few minor club dates in London.

Sims booked them cheaply, feeling publicity was more important than haggling for the highest rates. Nash would perform for thirty minutes, followed by Marley. They would do four shows a day, two morning assemblies and two in the afternoon. Neither Bob nor Nash made much money but English students got a glimpse of a current star and a greater one to come, as well as a welcome break from their studies. They got an enthusiastic reception from their young audiences. The assemblies, however, did not result in any bookings in more prestigious venues.

Tensions began to build between the successful star and the reggae musicians performing in his shadow. Nash loved reggae but the Wailers considered him a poor imitator. He did not become a Rasta, which the originators of the music considered essential. He infuriated the Wailers when he formed a backup band and labeled them The Sons of the Jungle. The name sounded like it catered to white stereotypes of black music. Nash added to the slight with a sign on his tour bus proclaiming him and his band as the

Kings of Reggae. Reggae was not jungle music, the Wailers groused, and Nash was surely not its king.

The band could not join Bob on stage during the school assemblies because officials had been slow processing their work visas. Just for the sake of performing, they decided to give a free concert at a small seaside town in the north of England. No one had ever heard of them. The audience did not know a thing about reggae, and the town was almost all white. But the music made instant converts of the crowd, which danced and shouted its way through the performance, with people throwing their hats onto the stage when the show ended. It was the one bright spot in an otherwise dismal trip.

Overall, Bob Marley and the Wailers helped Johnny Nash more than he helped them. Sims got them into a London studio to lay some tracks for Nash's next album *I Can See Clearly Now*. Nash sang three of Bob's songs on the album: "Stir It Up," "Guava Jelly," and "Comma Comma." The album became Nash's biggest hit. He scored hit singles with the title track and his cover of "Stir It Up."

By contrast, Bob got but a single record recorded through his CBS contract, "Reggae on Broadway." It sold poorly. Bob came to feel that his music poorly served his association with Nash and Sims. He liked Nash personally but did not think much of his music. "He's a nice guy but he doesn't know what reggae is," Bob said.

While Nash prospered, the Wailers struggled. In the shadow of Bob's failed CBS single, the band and Sims tried to piece together a European tour. That effort also failed. They had little money from their gigs and had to fight to keep a roof over their heads in the English cold. They bounced from a cellar in Surrey, to a cheap hotel and cold-water flat in London. Then Nash and Sims abruptly decided to fly to Florida to work on a new Nash project, leaving the Wailers abandoned and broke in a city that had brought them nothing but bad fortune.

Bob turned in desperation to a freelance publicity man named Brent Clarke, who had tried to promote "Reggae on Broadway" in London. Clarke went to the Chris Blackwell, owner and top producer of Island Records. They did not know it, but the miserable trip to a freezing island was about to turn into the biggest break in the career of Bob Marley and the Wailers.

five

The Wailers Catch Fire

B ob Marley and Chris Blackwell were men from different worlds. The owner of Island Records had led a life of material prosperity while Bob had traveled the hardscrabble road from Nine Miles to Trench Town.

Blackwell's family had made its fortune in products ranging from tea to canned goods. In the 1800s, they had gotten into the rum business, an extremely profitable decision, particularly in Jamaica, where rum was the preferred beverage of drinkers. Born in London on June 22, 1937, Blackwell had moved to Kingston when he was six months old. Although he spent most of his working life in England, he considered himself a Jamaican.

Blackwell's family did not push him to enter any profession. Their wealth was sufficient to allow him to live a life of ease, and neither of his parents worked. But Blackwell had the instincts of a businessman at an early age, as well as a rebellious streak. Sent to Harrow, a private school in

Chris Blackwell signed Bob Marley and the Wailers to his record label, Island Records. In this 2004 photo, Blackwell poses after receiving the Order of Jamaica honor for his contribution to the success of Jamaican music. *(Courtesy of AP Images/Collin Reid)*

England, he quickly got into trouble when he began selling liquor and cigarettes to his friends. He quit school in 1955. One of his first serious jobs was working as an assistant for the producer of the James Bond film *Dr. No.* He got the job through the author of the Bond books, Ian Fleming, who was a friend of the family. The producer of the movie offered Blackwell a tempting deal, the chance to work on an entire series of Bond movies. But Blackwell wanted to be his own boss. In 1962, he founded Island Records, Ltd. as a distributor for Jamaican records. He thought youngsters in England, weaned on rock and roll, would also buy the ska and rock steady sound coming from the island. His gamble paid off. Working-class white teens were drawn to black music, partly because they shared the feeling of being out-siders. Blackwell moved into mainstream rock, and by the time he met the Wailers, had made his own fortune by sign-ing such bands as Jethro Tull, Traffic, Fairport Convention, King Crimson, and Roxy Music.

Blackwell also distributed records from Jamaican produc-ers, including Leslie Kong and Coxsone Dodd. But it was difficult to determine who held the rights to songs, and how to distribute profits. Such confusion was part of the greater scheme of the producers, who wanted to keep most of the money for themselves. Even Lee "Scratch" Perry, who had helped the Wailers perfect their sound, was not above some dishonest shenanigans—such as claiming credit on one album for having written all of their songs. (On learning of the fraud, Bob confronted Perry and saw that the credit was corrected on future pressings of the album.)

What's more, the producers had helped spread the rumor that the Wailers were a difficult band to work with. Bob had sparked their anger when he attempted to start his own record label with Rita. Blackwell was prepared to have to deal with a headstrong and untrustworthy band when they arrived at his office.

The Wailers surprised Blackwell in several ways. They came dressed in clothes like those of manual laborers, heavy coats, jeans and work shoes. They did not even bring music to the first business meeting. "They were busted," Blackwell said. "Completely busted. And still they walked in the office like they were gods."

He thought they already looked like rock stars. The Wailers had more pride than money. They knew they could excite a crowd, having performed shows and made Jamaican hits for years. Far from being threatened by their ambition, as their previous producers had been, Blackwell admired it. As they talked around a round conference table at Island Records, he was already beginning to see the island's top band as a good gamble.

Blackwell offered to back the band while they made an album, for what he considered a modest sum, four thousand pounds. But for a reggae band from Jamaica, where artists received no advances and meager royalties, it was a splendid amount of cash. The deal was simple. The band would go to Jamaica and record whatever songs they chose. If Blackwell liked the record, he would distribute and promote it internationally.

This was the chance of a lifetime and the Wailers were determined not to blow it. They had been working two songs at a time their entire careers, issuing one top song and a "B" side for their Jamaican bosses. This would be their first long-playing album with all original material. It put them on a par with Blackwell's better-heeled rock clients and a rung above any other band in their home land. Other musicians were astonished and, no doubt, envious when the Wailers returned to Jamaica and news spread of their Island contract.

Bob had always been serious about his music. While Blackwell had not found the Wailers as hard to work with as he had feared, other musicians had found Bob to be a perfectionist. If anything, he became more demanding as they worked on the album. He would not even allow musicians to laugh while they were in the studio.

He had good reason to feel that time was too precious to be wasted. When the band began making the album in October of 1972, they were virtual unknowns outside of Jamaica. Bob was twenty-seven years old and had seen enough of the music business to realize he would have to make it soon, or not at all.

The core lineup now consisted of five members. The original three members, Bob, Peter, and Bunny, were joined by bass player Aston "Family Man" Barrett and Carlton "Carly" Barrett, both former welders who had played with the Upsetters. They recorded nine songs for the album. Peter wrote two of the tunes, "Stop That Train" and "400 Years." The other seven were Bob Marley compositions.

They worked at a furious pace, churning out the basic tracks in two weeks. They then worked on refining the sound, keeping the driving reggae bass line, adding a few rock flourishes to attract unschooled listeners. Blackwell flew to Jamaica while the band was working to hear a sample and loved it. When the Wailers finished the album later in the winter, Bob carried an eight-track tape of it back to Blackwell in London. The Island producer was sure they had a potential hit record. The Wailers debut album would be called *Catch a Fire*.

Blackwell set about adding a little more rock sound to the album, again tweaking the record to the tastes of the British and American listeners. He recruited studio musicians to add lead and bass guitar licks to the songs. Some of them had never heard of reggae before, and Bob and Blackwell worked closely together to make sure their contributions added to the album rather than detracted.

Bob did not resent making changes so *Catch a Fire* could build an audience beyond reggae's core fans. Some of what

Blackwell did was in keeping with the rock concert tradition, such as making songs longer. Bob got somewhat nervous when new licks were overdubbed, but he appreciated the fact Blackwell's musicians had talent too. When Wayne Perkins, an American musician from Alabama, first tried to play guitar for "Concrete Jungle," he could not even find the beat. After he got into rhythm, however, his guitar licks blended into the song beautifully. At the end of the session, Bob rushed out to congratulate Perkins.

Blackwell had another gimmick he applied for the promotion of *Catch a Fire*. Album sizes were huge in the 1970s, a little larger than a laptop screen on today's computers, which offered a great opportunity to put art on the covers. Blackwell had artists design the cover like a Zippo cigarette lighter, metallic colored, with a hinge at the top. When fans opened the hinge, they would find a "wick" inside with the record. The art for *Catch a Fire* has become a classic, revered by collectors of vinyl.

When it was released the album did not break into the top of American or British sales charts, but it attracted a lot of critical attention and most critics liked what they heard. It was enough to bolster Blackwell's confidence in the band, and the producer had enough money to keep backing the Wailers until mainstream rock and roll fans caught on to reggae. He sent the Wailers on a tour of British and American cities.

Blackwell had them play some London clubs so they could hone their *Catch a Fire* material before live audiences. They played the legendary British television show *The Old Grey Whistle Test,* another test of the reggae band's ability to prove itself to a rock audience. When they toured the United States, the Wailers mostly fronted for other established bands. They

Bob Marley and the Wailers perform on the set of *The Old Grey Whistle Test*. *(Courtesy of UrbanImage.tv/56 Hope Road Music/Adrian Boot)*

played Max's Kansas City in New York City with Bruce Springsteen and the E Street Band. Backstage Bob held a joyous reunion with his mother and the Booker family. He met his half-brother Richard, a boy in elementary school, who breathlessly told his reggae star relation of singing his songs in the first grade.

Not all the dates on the tour were so pleasant. When the Wailers played a roller skating rink in Las Vegas they opened for the popular rock and soul band Sly and the Family Stone. The Wailers were neither rock nor soul, so Sly's managers may have thought they were a safe bet to open the show. The Wailers, however, had the crowd on its feet and crying out for more by the time they finished. Upstaging the headline act is frowned upon for any front band and they were kicked off the tour after the Las Vegas date.

Growing pains put pressure on the childhood friends who had made the band what it was. Bunny dropped out, complaining that he could not stand the cold weather. Blackwell considered it an insane decision, one that could kill Bunny's career, but Bunny refused to change his mind. Joe Higgs, the Wailers' mentor who had taught them so much about the music business, took Bunny's place.

On top of that, Peter began to resent Bob's top billing. In the early days, the band had played many times as simply the Wailers, without the spotlight focused so much on Bob. Then Lee "Scratch" Perry had begun calling the group Bob Marley and the Wailers. Blackwell had yet to officially dub the group by that name, but did make it clear he considered Bob the leader. Peter could see the time coming when he might be considered just another sideman for Bob.

Some of his anger spilled over backstage. He ranted that Blackwell had plans to center the group around Bob, and demanded to know what right the British producer had to create such a hierarchy. "Who set one mon apart from Wailers an mek one t'ing become two separate t'ing?" he shouted.

Bob did not know the full extent of Peter's rage. Peter did not express it to Bob's face. No one can prepare themselves for sudden fame, and Bob was learning as he went along. So too, would the other Wailers, as their childhood bonds began to break apart under an international spotlight.

six

King of Reggae

By late 1973, Bob Marley's music rang from speakers throughout Europe and the United States. But he still did not own a home. He had lived in hotels, as well as basements and side rooms at studios, most of the time the Wailers were making their ascent to fame. Rita still lived in Trench Town.

Chris Blackwell had bought a home in Kingston at 56 Hope Road, hoping to put down some roots for his new reggae line. He called it Island House, after his record label. Bob began hanging out there and fell in love with the place. He made a deal with the producer to acquire the Hope Road house, saying he needed a headquarters to meet the press and hang out with his band mates. Blackwell was happy to make such a deal that would keep his new reggae star happy.

Island House was a mansion by Jamaican standards. A former plantation house, its rambling grounds were not far from

Bob Marley's house at 56 Hope Road *(Courtesy of UrbanImage.tv/Adrian Boot)*

the prime minister's house. It became the place to see and be seen as reggae rose in prominence during the 1970s.

Some of Bob's old Rasta friends thought Bob had sold out. A group of them complained to his face about it, and he told them they were welcome to come any time. Some of them took him up on the offer, while others grumbled and parted ways with him. The mix of visitors and hangers-on included island musicians, rock stars, would-be stars, and groupies. A visitor might run into Rastas smoking ganja, musicians jamming, British music industry people, or film stars. Some of Bob's female admirers created a great stain on his relationship with Rita. She lived with Bob's infidelities, as much as she resented them, and for the rest of their lives together, they had an open marriage—particularly from Bob's perspective.

Rita did not like living in Island House as much as Bob did, probably because she did not like to be confronted with his dalliances with other women. On the advice of a Rasta mentor, she bought a house in Bull Bay, just outside of Kingston. They had three children now. Cedella had been born in 1968, followed by Ziggy in 1970, and Stephen in 1972. Bob delighted in their company, playing soccer with them and teaching them to play dominoes. One of their favorite games was pretending their father was a monster out for their heads. Bob would put on a werewolf mask and chase his shrieking children through the house. He was a concerned father as well, checking with Rita to make sure they were staying in school and had everything they needed.

Everything had changed seemingly overnight for the man who had once had to share bites from a lunch cake with his band mates. At Island House, Bob Marley's staff, the other Wailers, and his Rasta brethren rubbed shoulders with producers, bodyguards, and groupies. Bob was clearly the king, setting the agenda for everyone else. Mornings began bright and early with a jog, with Bob setting the pace and deciding how far the group would run. Sometimes they would finish the morning run with a dip in Cane River Falls, allowing the Rastas to wash their dreadlocks and everyone to cleanse the sweat. Then they would trek to the market to buy fresh vegetables and fruit, including rice, sweet potatoes, papaya, carrots, mangoes, bananas, as well as fish. Bob's cook would prepare an ital feast, with every course determined by Rasta prescriptions for health and wellness. If the band had a recording session, it would take priority over every other afternoon activity. If not, he would organize soccer games.

Many nights turned into one long party. People smoked ganja and sang until the early hours of the morning. But Bob did not consider such gatherings as merely recreational. He considered the ganja a sacrament and often steered conversations toward Haile Selassie I and Rastafarianism. In his mind many of the evenings could be considered a Rasta "reasoning," a gathering where ganja is smoked and participants discuss issues of importance. For the British and American participants, the line between partying and religious observance must have seemed thin indeed.

Bob's religion gave his nightly gatherings a sacred mantle, something absent from the usual frolicking of rock stars. His love life, on the other hand, was very much in keeping with the rock star lifestyle. People competed for his attention, none more so than his many lovers.

He had groupies when he was famous only in Jamaica, and he frequently had liaisons with women other than Rita. Now his list of paramours included people who were more than just fans, women famed or accomplished in their own right. Esther Anderson, a well-known actor, was one of the first after *Catch a Fire*. Her acting achievements included playing opposite Oscar winner Sidney Poitier in the movie *A Warm December*. Bob's lawyer Diane Jobson became first a confidante, then a lover. One of his most passionate affairs was with the beautiful model Cindy Breakspeare.

Rita tried to keep her cool about the other women, although it was not easy. She had been in the music business long enough to know the temptations available to famous musicians. But sometimes she lost her temper with the mistresses. She brought her children one morning when she went to see Bob at Island House, only to be met by Esther Anderson at the porch. Anderson refused to wake Bob, then began to insult Rita as though she were an intruder. Anderson crossed a line when she brought Bob and Rita's children into the argument.

"Bob needs a career, and you need to stop breeding and let him find a life!" Anderson yelled. The confrontation escalated into a furious shouting match between Bob, Esther, and Rita. Rita cursed them both and left. Bob later went to the Bull Bay house and they made up.

Rita continued coming to Island House, he continued to support her and the children, and she kept singing backup with the Wailers. She reluctantly accepted his mistresses, later writing that when Breakspeare bore Bob a child, she was happy for the two of them. Bob had helped her break out of Trench Town. As far as the music was concerned, the two were soul mates until Bob died. She never stopped believing in the power of reggae and Rasta. "It was like musical warfare—good against evil!" she wrote. Overall, she was happier than she had ever been. She did even the score, though, taking lovers of her own, including Jamaican soccer star Owen "Tacky" Stewart. In 1974, she bore a fourth child for Bob, a girl named Stephanie.

Both Blackwell and the Wailers knew they had to follow up *Catch a Fire* with another album that would keep the public's attention. They went back to the studio to work on a release that would be called *Burnin'.* Bob had shown he could accommodate rock licks with the island's roots reggae on *Catch a Fire.* He was less compromising about Jamaican rage against oppression. The song "Burnin' and Lootin' Tonight" begins with lyrics about waking up in prison and confronting one's jailers. The anger boils over with a threat of mob violence: "That's why we gonna be/Burnin' and a-lootin' tonight." "Get Up, Stand Up" urged resistance: "Get Up, Stand Up, stand up for your right/Get Up, Stand Up, don't give up the fight." The title of "I Shot the Sheriff" speaks for itself.

Bob poses with his wife, Rita, Rita's daughter Sharon, whom Bob adopted, and their children, Ziggy, Cedella, and Steven. *(Courtesy of UrbanImage.tv/ Trax/Ossie Hamilton)*

Rock and roll had begun with a rebellious attitude in the 1950s, in a time when Elvis Presley's hip gyrations were considered too sexual to be shown on television. The Wailers were taking the rebellion in a different direction, showing their fans the face of Jamaican discontent. *Burnin'* became a huge critical and commercial success. Other rock stars praised the new music. Former Beatle Paul McCartney declared reggae to be "where it's at." Folk singer Paul Simon went to Kingston to record his next album. Mick Jagger of the Rolling Stones and his bride Bianca hired the reggae band The Greyhounds to perform at their wedding. The Wailers had reached the peak of success, the place they had dreamed of since their Trench Town days.

All was not well within the band, however. Bunny still refused to tour, and Blackwell berated him for it, warning that he would become a nobody if he remained stubborn on the issue. Bunny held his ground, insisting he would never go on the road. Peter had intensely disliked Blackwell since the first tour, and his ill temper

Bunny Livingston *(Courtesy of UrbanImage. tv/Trax/Ossie Hamilton)*

boiled into rage as he began to suspect the producer was trying to divide the group. Shouting matches disrupted jamming and recording sessions. On one occasion, Peter even threatened Blackwell with a machete.

On a creative level, Peter and Bunny wanted to establish themselves as musicians beyond the Wailers. Blackwell thought the group needed to cement its reputation as the first international reggae superstar band. When Peter approached the producer about making a solo album, Blackwell refused to help. He argued such a record would only undercut the Wailers. Peter quit the Wailers in early 1974, just as a new album was being planned. He made a recording deal with CBS and left for New York to begin work. He set up his own record label, and his visits to Bob's house became rare. Bunny did not make as clean a break. He continued to hang out at Island House, staying close to Bob and keeping their friendship, but he also quit the Wailers.

Rita saw the pain Bob felt at losing his closest band mates. She thought it hurt him more than it had Peter or Bunny. "He took it very, very hard," she wrote. "He felt hurt and abandoned, and he never stopped thinking about it; that sadness was always a part of him. They had been so young when they got together as the Wailers, and it was like being deserted by your brothers . . ."

Bob's attitude toward himself and every other group of musicians he played with thereafter changed. He began to see himself more or less the way Blackwell did. After the early months of 1974, he began to tell people that whomever he happened to be singing with were the Wailers. In other words, the Wailers consisted of anyone he said it did.

Bob also began working with a new manager. Don Taylor had been born in Jamaica and got his start doing odd jobs for musicians. He moved to the United States in the 1950s, where he became an assistant for Motown artist Chuck Jackson. He later took a job as a valet for Little Anthony and the Imperials and parlayed that position into becoming their manager. He proved himself a capable director of other people's careers when the formerly popular group went through a tough period on the pop charts. Although they had not had a hit in years,

Taylor got the Imperials prestigious bookings at the Empire Room of the Waldorf-Astoria in New York and in Las Vegas. Soon after, he returned to his native country.

Taylor introduced himself to Bob in the brashest manner possible. He went to Island House with the intention of meeting the reggae superstar. Told that Bob was asleep, Taylor walked up to his bedroom and woke him. Bob was amused by Taylor's nerve and after a short conversation became convinced this man's gutsy style might work well in business negotiations. He hired Taylor on the spot. His new manager soon showed his skill, negotiating a more favorable contract for his client before the next album was released.

Next Bob had to put together a new group of Wailers. He recruited his wife, along with two other women who had been recording since the days everyone was working for Coxsone Dodd. Marcia Griffiths had cut two records that went on to become hits, "Electric Boogie" and "Young, Gifted and Black." Judy Mowatt was a former member of the Gaylettes, one of Dodd's female soul bands. The three had sung together in Kingston clubs, proving their ability to get a crowd on its feet. They formed a distinct unit within the band called the I-Threes. Guitarist Al Anderson and keyboardist Tyrone Downie completed the new lineup.

The new album was called *Natty Dread* and it became an instant classic, a hit with both the critics and the public. It contained tunes that have become the most popular of Bob's work, ranging from the upbeat "Lively Up Yourself" to "No Woman, No Cry," a song that alternates between harsh memories of poverty in Trench Town to a verse of reconciliation: "Ev'rything's gonna be alright." The band toured Europe and

America, playing before frenzied crowds and building an ever-expanding fan base. *Natty Dread* sealed Bob's reputation as the foremost star of reggae.

A show in Kingston in October of 1974 helped heal some old wounds. The Wailers performed as part of a double bill with soul singer Stevie Wonder, one of the most popular American performers in Jamaica. Wonder was the headline act, but he invited the Wailers back onstage to perform with his Wonderlove band. Wonder provided a driving piano beat to the Wailers' performance of "I Shot the Sheriff." Most importantly, Peter and Bunny joined Bob on stage. It was a happy, poignant, reminder of the past.

Bob's success was making him more than a musician in the eyes of Jamaicans. He became a spokesman for the Rasta movement and a national hero. Even politicians began seeking his favor—and that is when some of his worst troubles started.

Island House sat in one of the most posh neighborhoods in Kingston, close to the home of Prime Minister Michael Manley. Manley began to discreetly drop by Island House, joining Bob's entourage for evenings at a time. He enjoyed Bob's charisma as much as any of the others, but he also sought to use it to the advantage of his People's National Party.

Manley possessed some charisma of his own. He came from an elite family, the son of former Premier Norman Manley. Nonetheless, he had built his image as a friend of the people, supporting trade unions and backing several socialist type reforms that sought a more equitable distribution of wealth.

Manley won a resounding victory over the more conservative incumbent Prime Minister Hugh Shearer in 1972. Once

Michael Manley served as the prime minister of Jamaica during a period of intense political rivalries and violent protests. *(Courtesy of AP Images)*

in office, he kept an informal appearance, often wearing a bush jacket instead of a suit and tie, and allowing members of parliament to attend sessions in informal attire. He also sought closer alliances with other leftist world leaders, including Prime Minister Pierre Trudeau of Canada and Cuban dictator Fidel Castro. His ties with Castro cast him as a potential communist in the halls of power in the United States, where many political leaders viewed all world politics in the context of the struggle between U.S. capitalism and Soviet Union Communism.

Rumors spread that the U.S. Central Intelligence Agency (CIA) was determined to oust Manley—and Manley believed the rumors. To a degree, U.S. suspicions that Manley would lead Jamaica closer to the Soviet Union were accurate. He would later push for better relations with the Russians as a way to protest imperialism and colonialism, both historically associated with the enslavement of black Jamaicans.

In the 1976 elections, Manley faced a determined rival in Edward Seaga. Born in Boston to parents of Arab and Scottish origins, Seaga had been a record producer in the 1960s and had owned West Indies Records Limited. He had even organized a troupe of ska performers for the 1964 World's Fair in New York. Seaga had once been thought to be a liberal, but he had become more conservative by the time he became a candidate for prime minister. As head of the Jamaican Labor Party (JLP), he promoted a stronger bond with the U.S., a break in relations with Castro, and an end to the levies Manley had imposed on aluminum ore, a measure that had angered U.S. corporations.

The rivalry between Manley and Seaga had turned ugly and violent by the time Manley began visiting Island House. Both candidates had enlisted Kingston's street thugs, arming rival factions of hooligans. Anger spurred by poverty had been enough to spark violent outbursts by the Rude Boys in the past. Now they had a political feud and party-supplied weapons to add to the dangerous mix.

Marley did not like to get involved in politics. But his lyrics touched on the themes of politics, because Bob had always been concerned about the struggle between the haves and have-nots. The music of *Natty Dread* had stated some of his philosophy. In "Them Belly Full (But We Hungry)," he had warned of an uprising by the desperate, with the lyrics "Them belly full but we hungry/A hungry mob is a angry mob." *Rastaman Vibration,* released in 1976, expressed some of the same protests. "War" set to music a speech Haile Selassie I had delivered to the United Nations. Marley sang "That until the basic human rights are equally/Guaranteed to all, without regard to race/Dis a war." The fact he could deliver such strident messages through the sweet melodies and rhythms of reggae making his overall message sound hopeful, was one of Bob's great gifts.

Manley hoped to use Marley's talent in the upcoming election. Members of Manley's People's National Party approached Bob about performing a free concert in December. They assured him the event would not be slanted toward either party. It would instead be an attempt to bring peace and unity as the democratic process proceeded.

Bob's partners and friends did not like the idea. Chris Blackwell was highly suspicious of Manley's motives and Rita thought it was dangerous. Bob approached Peter and Bunny with the idea of uniting the original Wailers at the event. Both refused. Bunny dismissed the idea as just more politics. Peter went a step farther, saying he did not even want the peace Manley claimed he advocated, but equality and justice.

In the end, Bob ignored their advice. He agreed to perform and the date was set for December 5. The concert for political peace would be called "Smile Jamaica."

seven

Blood for Peace

I n late November, days before the "Smile Jamaica" concert,
Bob had a nightmare. He could not see anything but shad-
ows, but he could hear guns firing and smell gunpowder.
He was not the only Wailer having nightmares.

Judy Mowatt of the I-Threes also began having bad dreams.
The night after Bob and the Wailers wrote the song "Smile
Jamaica" for the concert, she dreamed she saw a newspaper
and read the headline "Bob Got Shot for a Song." In another
dream, she saw bullets flying toward a rooster surrounded by
chickens. The bullets missed the rooster but hit the chickens.
The symbols were clear enough, as she saw it: Bob was the
rooster and the chickens were the I-Threes.

Rastas often interpret dreams as prophecy. The dangers
the Wailers faced in doing the concert, though, would have
rattled anyone's nerves. Michael Manley's PNP and Edward
Seaga's JLP had lit the fuse on a powder keg by bringing
armed gunmen into their parties. "When it was time for

politics, the party bosses would hand out guns and say 'Go kill the opposition,'" Rita Marley wrote.

Rumors spread that Marley was in league with the incumbent party, perhaps because Prime Minister Manley had first approached Bob about the concert. Of course, he was in league with no one, having agreed to perform more in accordance with his philosophy than anyone's politics. Since the days he had sung "Simmer Down," he had urged Jamaicans to cease killing each other. With his faith in music, he had believed the Wailers' songs could quiet people's fears during the tense election. But the shooters recruited by the parties did not share Bob's idealism. In Trench Town, they even fired into school houses during their battles.

Regulars at Hope Road began seeing strangers in the house. A group of PNP vigilantes called the Echo Squad set up a

In the days leading up to the "Smile Jamaica" concert, gunmen guarded Bob's house at 56 Hope Road twenty-four hours a day. *(Courtesy of UrbanImage. tv/Adrian Boot)*

ring around Marley's home, guarding it twenty-four hours a day with automatic rifles. The free and easy atmosphere vanished to be replaced by a paramilitary presence. Echo Squad refused entrance to almost everyone but the band.

On Friday, December 3, two days before the concert, Chris Blackwell and some associates met with Bob's agent Don Taylor at the Kingston Sheraton Hotel. After the business meeting, Taylor drove to Island House. He failed to notice that two white Datsuns carrying seven men had pulled out behind his car. The Datsuns followed Taylor to Bob's home, where the manager got out and went inside. At about 8:45 p.m., Wailer percussionist Seeco Patterson looked out a window and saw something strange. The Echo Squad was nowhere to be seen.

About thirty minutes later, Bob was standing in his kitchen eating a piece of grapefruit, while talking to Taylor. A shot rang out and he dropped the fruit. The manager walked up to Bob just in time for a second shot to enter the kitchen, followed by a flurry of gunfire. Taylor did not know it then, but he had managed to shield his client from the bullets meant to kill him. Four shots hit Taylor in the upper thighs, and a fifth lodged at the base of his spine. Only one of the bullets hit their intended target, grazing Bob's chest and lodging in his left elbow.

Rita had just left the house and gotten in her yellow Volkswagen to drive home when the shooting started. Two young men were in the car with her, friends from Bull Bay. She looked back to see the gunman who had fired at Marley and Taylor, then floored the gas pedal while her two passengers ducked. Shots crashed through the windows, one of them creasing her head. She slumped over the wheel. Several gunmen looked in, saw the blood coming from her head and ran off, satisfied she was dead.

The assassination attempt showed the recklessness running rampant through that election year. Fortunately for everyone involved, the assassins had been poorly chosen. They fired almost randomly and left prematurely. The gunman who shot Marley and Taylor was only sixteen. When ambulances arrived medical attendants found Bob walking around the house in a bloodstained khaki outfit. They rushed him and Taylor to University College Hospital. Taylor was by far the most seriously injured and was later flown to a Miami hospital for removal of a bullet near his spine. Bob was treated and released. Rita was released the next day.

Under police escort, he was taken to a secret encampment in the Blue Mountains. The shootings threw the Wailers' plans to perform into doubt. The band, along with its handlers, spent much of Saturday discussing whether the Wailers should perform. Guards hid in trees around the camp, keeping watch for intruders. The Rastas held a reasoning session with Bob and his band mates. Some urged him to go on with the performance, to show that his message would not be stopped by violence. By the end of the day Saturday, he had still not reached a decision. The whole island knew of the attempt on his life, but 50,000 people nonetheless arrived at National Heroes Circle hours before the concert. Members of Third World, one of the opening acts, told Bob they intended to play. Over a walkie-talkie, he listened to the crowd cheering Third World. He asked for a car to be sent downtown to collect the Wailers. They would play the Smile Jamaica concert.

When an MC announced the Wailers were en route to Heroes Circle, a thunderous din rose from the crowd. The audience had swelled to 80,000 by the time the Wailers took the stage.

Bob assured those gathered that he was there for them, not the politicians. "I jus' wanted to play fe de love of de people," he said.

His injury had left him unable to play the guitar and he told the crowd he would be singing only—and then launched into "War," the musical reworking of the Selassie speech calling for militant defense of human rights. His song's message was clear: "We find it necessary and we know we shall win/ As we are confident in the victory/ Of good over evil, good over evil, good over evil."

Revived by the audience's enthusiasm, Bob decided to go for the whole show. Rita joined him on stage, her scarf covering the bandages on her head and Bob pulled up his shirt to show the people his wounds. Near the end of the set, Bob began to pantomime the cowboy bravado of gunmen,

Bob Marley performs at the "Smile Jamaica" concert. (*Courtesy of AP Images*)

pulling his hands from his side and aiming his fingers like gun barrels. Enjoying this joke on his would-be killers, he threw his dreadlocks back in laughter.

The concert became one of the most memorable of Marley's career. But Rita saw him during the days and months following the concert, and was convinced the attack had changed him. She knew they had changed her. "But now he was frightened in a way he hadn't been, because even though he had been warned by these gunmen that they were out to get him, he never thought they would try," she wrote. "And all of us knew that with no trouble at all they could succeed, and how little it would take for them to try again."

eight
Fame and Scandal

Soon after the shooting, Bob left Jamaica. Michael Manley won the election and basked in his landslide victory while Marley recovered from the attack. Bob took time to let his arm heal enough to play again, staying for a while with his mother Cedella in the United States, then traveling to London, where he set up a place for the Wailers to meet and practice at Oakley Street in Chelsea. Rita may have been right about the spiritual and psychological toll of the attack—he would stay away from Jamaica for more than a year.

But he did not let the attack affect his music. By February of 1977, he was back in studio with the Wailers, turning out new songs at a rapid clip. In a month's time, they had twenty-four tunes, enough for two albums. It was the beginning of one of the most prolific outpourings of Bob's career, with five albums hitting the charts in three years.

In his early days of touring, London had seemed a cold and indifferent city. It felt a good bit more friendly now that he had more money, a recording contract and legions of reggae fans. He also had the full attention of the press, but this turned out to be a mixed blessing, particularly the attention he got from the scandal-hungry tabloids.

Bob had some love affairs he would have preferred to keep secret, including his relationship with model Cindy Breakspeare, whose also had a flourishing career. She racked up beauty queen crowns almost as rapidly as Bob and the Wailers turned out albums. Bob found her irresistible, as she did him, and he wrote the love song "Turn Your Lights Down

Bob had a relationship with beauty queen Cindy Breakspeare (middle). *(Courtesy of Getty Images/Central Press)*

Low" for her. No more than they could resist each other, could the press resist following and photographing them. The reggae king and the beauty queen made for wonderfully salacious stories. There was a movie deal in the works for Breakspeare, a film titled *Beauty and the Beast.* Typical of the tabloids' treatment of the pair was a photo with a caption that borrowed the movie title to describe them.

In her biography, Rita rationalized that many Jamaican men have affairs outside of marriage. "He himself still gave me the manners and the respect to a certain level," she wrote. "I didn't think I should disrupt his relationships, though sometimes the situation was painful and I couldn't understand what was going on. But I got tired of standing in the way, and as long as I was respected, given whatever I needed financially, and whatever the kids needed was there, I let him be."

Bob seemed much like the average rock star in such matters as his dalliances with Breakspeare and other women, as well as his recently acquired taste for material pleasures. He drove expensive cars, joking that his BMW stood for Bob Marley and the Wailers. He enjoyed spending money and giving it away to old Rasta friends. But his spirituality still ran deep.

Shortly after he arrived in London, his Rasta contacts set up a meeting with Ethiopian Crown Prince Asfa Wossen. Marley and the prince spent considerable time discussing the fate of the Rasta idol Haile Selassie I. A widespread famine had dimmed Selassie's popularity with his own people. He had been overthrown by a military coup in 1974 and placed under house arrest. On August 28, 1975, the government announced the emperor had died of complications after prostate surgery.

His doctor denied the account, setting the stage for a pro-longed controversy. There were those in Ethiopia who said he was suffocated by his enemies in his sleep. At the time of the meeting between Marley and Wossen, some Rastas refused to believe he was dead, a claim that has persisted to this day.

The two men were about to part when Wossen announced he had a gift for Marley. Wossen took a ring from his pocket and gave it to him. The ring had a figure of the Lion of Judah on it, and Wossen explained that it had belonged to Emperor Selassie. When Wossen put it on his finger Marley could hardly believe this was happening. This was the ful-

fillment of the dream he had in his mother's house in Delaware so many years before. He wore it for the rest of his life, swearing it was so powerful that it burned his finger sometimes.

In May of 1977, *Exodus,* the first album from the London sessions, was released.

Bob proudly wore Selassie's ring for the rest of his life. *(Courtesy of UrbanImage.tv/56 Hope Road Music/Adrian Boot)*

The title came from the biblical book describing the deliverance of Jewish slaves from Egypt. The album soared to the top of the charts, spinning off three hit singles, "Exodus," "Waiting in Vain," and "Jammin.'" Island Records set up a tour of Europe and the States.

Island's publicity department also arranged for Bob and the Wailers to be seen with the famous and wealthy, and to make themselves available to journalists. Bob delivered what the public relations people wanted, in his own fashion. When Bianca Jagger, wife of Rolling Stones front man Mick Jagger, saw Bob in Paris, she ran up and kissed him. Bob professed not to know who she was. At a Los Angeles party for celebrities and studio bosses, the other Wailers arrived in limousines attired in tuxedos and formal dress. Bob showed up fashionably late after dinner at an Ethiopian restaurant, climbing out of a truck and mingling with the crowd in jeans, his shirt half buttoned. This was the Bob Marley his fans so loved—disdainful of button-down convention and business demands.

A seemingly insignificant event that would turn out to have tragic consequences happened on the first stop of the *Exodus* tour. In June, Bob took a little time off in Paris to play soccer with journalists. One of them threw a nasty tackle on him, injuring his right toe. He saw a doctor, who advised him to stay off the foot. A second visit to a doctor in London resulted in a different diagnosis. The doctor in London discovered that he had melanoma, an aggressive cancer of the skin and informed him the best course would be to amputate the toe.

Bob was distraught. The Rasta religion took a dim view of amputation. A coincidence of Rasta religious dates may have deepened his dread. Much had been made of the "clash of sevens" for 1977, and some dreadlocked prophets had already predicted disastrous events. Rasta poet Joseph Hill had written a song called "Two Sevens Clash" which suggested an upheaval in Jamaica. Much of the sevens imagery came from the Bible's Book of Revelation, which foretells a seven-headed dragon, seven visitations of God's wrath, seven plagues, and so on. The London doctor delivered the melanoma diagnosis on July 7, 1977.

After sustaining a foot injury while playing soccer, Bob visited a doctor who discovered cancer in his toe. (*Courtesy of AP Images*)

On a more worldly level, Bob worried about what an amputation would do to his stage persona. He always danced about the stage during the shows, along with many members of his audience. He fumed to Rita. " 'How would I go on stage?' " he demanded. 'They won't stay looking at a crippled man!'"

Bob sought a second opinion in Miami. An orthopedic surgeon there gave him what appeared the far better option, a skin graft to heal the afflicted toe. Bob jumped at the chance to save his toe. The doctor performed the graft, and told Bob it had succeeded.

His brush with cancer caused Bob to consider his mortality more deeply. After his operation, he went to the house his mother still kept in Delaware, along with the home he had bought for her in Miami. He talked with her about the Bible, about Rasta and Haile Selassie I. He told her of his encounter with Crown Prince Wossen and the gift of the ring, the fulfillment of the prophetic dream he had many years earlier in the same house. One day when she was away visiting a relative, he shocked some of his friends with a strange prediction. They were talking about Jesus, whom Bob claimed had died at the age of thirty-six. He told them he would die at the same age.

"Next year 1978," he said. "Me be t'irty-t'ree in February. From dat month, t'ings tek dere course from den." His buddies tried to reassure him, saying he was far too young to die. When he insisted on his gloomy prediction, they wrote it off to lingering depression from his illness.

His physical problems took their toll on his career. His convalescence forced the cancellation of the American leg of the *Exodus* tour. Disappointed fans can be slow to forgive their idols, and sales of *Exodus* sputtered in the U.S. Bob and the Wailers took a second hit when the next songs from the London sessions were released on an album titled *Kaya,* which got sour reviews from some critics, most notably in the *Rolling Stone,* which had praised their previous Wailers releases. Reviewer Lester Bangs called it "quite possibly the blandest set of reggae music I have ever heard." Rock critics who preferred a militant style of reggae had no patience with an album containing so many love ballads.

Fortunately for Bob and the Wailers, fans disregarded the notices. *Kaya* rose to Number Four in Britain, soaring in sync with two hot singles, "Satisfy My Soul" and "Is This Love." Bob was not bulletproof, but his bond with his fans remained strong.

Jamaica's most famous musician was doing far better than its politicians. Unemployment had soared during Manley's current term, while the government treasury teetered on the edge of bankruptcy. In the face of economic stress, violence again broke out, not only between the rival parties but within the ranks of the People's National Party (PNP). PNP gunmen shot one another in intraparty disputes.

Once again, the two parties sought a musical healing. Spokesmen for the rival parties approached Bob while he was in the U.S. to ask him to appear at a peace concert. Given the risk and injury he had taken on for the sake of his country at the "Smile Jamaica" event, the request might have seemed above the call of duty. But he agreed to perform at the event billed as the "One Love Peace Concert." Other popular acts, including Peter Tosh, would accompany Bob and the Wailers on the bill.

In February of 1978, just after *Kaya's* release, Bob's plane touched down in Kingston. He led several thousand fans in Rasta chants at the National Heroes Circle Stadium that night. Continuing the chain of seemingly bad signs, two earthquake tremors shook the city before the ceremony ended.

This time, though, no bullets flew. The concert went off without a hitch, except a few uncomfortable moments for the politicians. Tosh chided Prime Minister Manley for failure to legalize marijuana, which he had implied he would do during his 1976 campaign. The former Wailer gleefully undercut the premise of the concert, announcing "Me don' wan' peace, me wan' equality!" Marley offered the men whose parties had engaged in such bloodshed little quarter. During the band's performance of "Jamming," he called on Manley and PNP leader Edward Seaga to come on stage and shake hands. It was not an easy moment for the nervously smiling rivals, but Marley considered it fair play, considering all they had asked of him.

"We got them two big people together," he said. "Rasta bring them together. Same people them fight bring them together."

Having once again delivered what Jamaica's leaders wanted, Bob resumed touring. He and the Wailers traveled worldwide, going onstage in Europe, North America, New Zealand, Australia and Japan. Bob did not have to compose anything from scratch to make their next album. Island released *Babylon by Bus,* recorded in Paris in June the previous year, the same tour stop where Bob took the soccer tackle that revealed cancer in his foot.

Fans had bought the music even when reviewers panned it. This time, though, the critics did an about face. *Rolling Stone,* which had so caustically dismissed *Kaya,* raved about the concert album. "*Babylon by Bus* reverberates with an awesome faith in the power of love in all its difficult and rewarding forms," reviewer Timothy White wrote. "It's a statement that Bob Marley and the Wailers have been building up to for some time, and it explodes here with a humanity and an urgency as potent as any of the band's previous darker calls to arms."

Bob was beyond the point where he had to worry much about what critics said. He wrote and performed what he chose, including some very personal material on which he and Rita collaborated for their children. Four of his children joined to form the Melody Makers and released a song called "Children Playing in the Streets," about the sad lives of impoverished Kingston kids. Sharon, age fourteen, sang with the group, as did Cedella, twelve, Ziggy, eleven, and Stephen, five. They donated their profits to the United Nations Children's Fund.

Those who liked Bob's militant side got their money's worth in the summer of 1979. Early in the year, he and the Wailers began laying down the tracks to an album with the working title of *Black Survival* at his new twenty-four track Tuff Gong studio at Hope Road. The album was uncompromising in its messages about violence and revolution, with "Ambush in the Night" recalling the assassination attempt. Its odes to what Bob Marley considered black people's continent of destiny ranged from the back-to-Africa call of "Africa Unite," to the apocalyptic vision of "Ride Natty Ride," with its warning of an all consuming blaze: "And it's the fire, it's the fire, fire/ Burning down everything." The album was released under the title *Survival.*

The Wailers launched a forty-seven stop North American tour for the new album at New York's Apollo Theatre in October. The schedule pushed the band to the limit, calling for almost a concert a day. Some of those closest to Bob noticed a weariness that he had never shown before. In his early days living at Hope Road, he could outlast every partier and late night Rastaman, but those times were gone. The sleep he lost began to show on him, and he caught colds easily.

In 1979, Bob Marley and the Wailers toured North America to promote their newest album, *Survival*. *(Courtesy of UrbanImage.tv/56 Hope Road Music/ Adrian Boot)*

Early the next year, he lost one of his longstanding professional relationships when he fired his manager Don Taylor. The trouble began in the African nation of Gabon, where the Wailers planned to play a concert for the birthday of President Omar Bongo. Bob was angered to find out that only the country's privileged elite would be allowed to attend. After the show, he accused Taylor of shorting the band of $20,000 of the proceeds and gave him the ax.

He began to show signs of impending dread. Soon after getting back from Africa, the band returned to the Tuff Gong studio in Jamaica to record an album to be called *Uprising.* One afternoon, during the recording of the song "Could You Be Loved," guitarist Junior Marvin unplugged his guitar and started to leave. He meant no affront. He simply thought band mate Al Anderson had taken over the lead guitar part.

"Don' leave!" Bob called. "Me don' 'ave much time!" Anderson heard an urgency in Bob's voice that indicated he might have been talking about something of more importance than studio minutes.

The finished work brought about an exchange between Marley and Chris Blackwell that crossed the usual lines between artist and producer. When he heard the initial tracks, Blackwell bluntly told Bob that he thought there was more to the album than came across in the first take. Bob came back with two more songs, "Coming in From the Cold" and "Redemption Song." The latter became one of Bob's most enduring ballads, evoking both images of slave ships and a promise of deliverance. Bob played guitar for a folk style song that some have compared to the work of Bob Dylan. "Redemption Song" is not reggae, but it is a song that touches Bob's creative core as much as any of his reggae hits.

Everything went fine in the first days after *Uprising's* release. It was a hit, of course, as Bob's loyal fans quickly grabbed it from record store shelves. The band staged a highly successful European tour, with the 1 million fans they played for setting a record for the continent. Then it was on to the United States, where Bob and the Wailers first played Boston, then New York. They played two shows at Madison Square Garden, then had a short layover before flying to Pittsburgh. On Sunday morning after the second show, Bob decided to go jogging in Central Park with his friend, soccer player Alan "Skilly" Cole.

As the two rounded a pond, Bob's neck froze in paralysis. He could not speak, nor move his head, as he toppled to the ground.

The band flew to Pittsburg, while Bob went to a neurologist. The diagnosis brought the worst of news. The fall had been caused by a stroke, set off by a brain tumor. When

Rita visited him in his hotel room, she found him looking exhausted and frail. He told her what the doctor had said, and she burst into tears. She urged him to cancel the tour. He refused.

Bob played the show in Pittsburgh as planned and delivered for his fans. He performed his hits and even came back on for two encores. Pittsburgh fans could not have known how bittersweet an occasion they had witnessed, for their city's show would be the last of Bob Marley's life.

nine
Fading Light

Bob resisted canceling the Tuff Gong Uprising, to the point of playing worn out and sick. He was determined to keep going, but bad news from the doctors kept coming.

He went to physicians in Miami and New York. The terminal diagnosis finally came from doctors at New York's Memorial Sloan-Ketting Center on October 7, 1980. They informed Bob that cancer had invaded his brain, lungs, and stomach, and was still spreading. They gave him three months to live.

He quickly took on the standard regimen for cancer patients, including radiation and chemotherapy. He settled a spiritual matter when he was baptized, at Rita's behest, into the Ethiopian Orthodox Church, becoming a Christian Rasta on November 4. He took the name Berhane Selassie.

Bob went from one clinic to the next in search of a cure, traveling from Sloan-Kettering in New York to Cedars of

Lebanon in Miami, to a Mexican treatment center famed for celebrity clientèle, then back again to New York.

When word of his disease leaked out to the media, Bob faced an additional stress. Published reports began to tell of his imminent death and, naturally, these stories worsened his depression. Rita began trying to shield him from the news. A Jamaican doctor, Dr. Carl "Pee Wee" Fraser, suggested he try a radical therapy in Europe, far from the United States media's glare. Dr. Josef Issels of Germany had built a practice based on a holistic approach to the treatment of hopeless cases. Fraser suggested Bob go to Issels's clinic in Rottach-Egern, a Bavarian mountain town.

Bob agreed. While a cover story had him traveling to Ethiopia to be treated for exhaustion, Bob instead went to Issels' clinic. He was accompanied by a small entourage consisting of Rita, his mother Cedella, his lawyer Diane Jobson, Dr. Fraser and a few friends.

Issels's45 compound stood on a gentle incline of terraces. The brisk mountain air opened the lungs and was braced by shaded places to run or walk. Bob saw Dr. Issels, a broad-shouldered man, who told his patient of his confidence in their therapy as soon as they met. "We can make it work," he said.

Bob's belief in a whole body approach had compelled him to reject the London doctor who had advised amputation when his toe first showed melanoma. It was a doctrine shared by Dr. Issels, who had made his fame advocating the treatment of the cancer by treating the whole body. Issel believed any treatment that damaged the human immune system for the objective of driving out the cancer was bad. He believed in exercise, blood transfusions, and a diet which

Dr. Josef Issels *(Courtesy of Popperfoto/Alamy)*

dovetailed strongly with the *ital* cooking of the Rastas. This was a medical tactic that supported Bob's own beliefs about good health.

Issels's methods were controversial. A 1970 British Broadcast Corporation report noted the German doctor's central claim "that a healthy body cannot develop cancer. Therefore, he believes that the entire metabolism of the body must be treated . . . To him, cancer is a local symptom of an entire body deficiency, a sort of red alert that the whole body is in danger." This was not a view supported by most researchers.

In keeping with his belief that cancer was a symptom of the whole body gone awry, Issels took control of every aspect of his patients' life. He would even order patients to fast during certain cycles of the treatment, a radical strategy indeed for someone wasting away, as Bob was.

Bob's trademark dreadlocks were among the first casualties of the cancer treatment. He wore a skullcap with Rasta colors over his head, asking his friends and children if he looked ugly, and they assured him he did not. He kept up a brave front, playing with a soccer ball as much as his frail body would let him and even attempting to play music. But he would have seizures if he kicked the ball for too long and could not play the guitar for long. He felt all the more intensely the bullet still lodged in his arm from the failed assassination attempt.

Bob refused to make a will. "Who ready fe dead?" he protested when approached about the subject. Others, however, saw Bob's light fading. He would frequently go into convulsions, shaking through his entire body, his eyes peeled back to the whites, while an old Trench Town friend named Bird held him.

Every so often he would undertake some task of endurance to prove to himself, or someone else, that he still had inner strength. He walked once to the top of a small mountain, accompanied by his German translator. When he tried to repeat the feat with his mother Cedella Booker, though, he had a seizure as he tried to cross a pontoon bridge. Gradually, he and his friends learned the folly of trying to pretend all was as it was before. More and more, he began to fill his days with quiet activities, reading the Bible with his mother, or watching a television in his cottage. His favorite things to watch were Bruce Lee karate movies. Letters piled up from fans who had read the dire news in the papers or seen reports on television. Everyone, it seemed, had advice on how their idol could best be treated for his disease.

Bob's friends did their best to keep Bob's spirits up, but their own were flagging. Chris Blackwell flew in and listened to song tapes with his top reggae star and even slept on a spare bed in Bob's room to keep him company during the long nights. Bob's mother began to snap at some of his Jamaican entourage, suspecting they were only after his money. She later wrote that she heard them speculating on whether her dying son would repay their kindness by buying them expensive cars.

Issels made no definite promises that he would survive, but managed to keep Bob hanging on into the early months of 1981, defying all other doctors' predictions. On February 6, some of his friends and fellow musicians held a small birthday party for him. It was far from the raucous events which had once enlivened Hope Road almost every night, but it brought Bob some comfort. He seemed strong and alert as they watched a television show with highlights of World Cup matches.

Eventually, however, Issels exhausted all the treatment methods in his unconventional arsenal. In early spring, he announced Bob could go home. He did not need to add that he was sending the patient home to die.

Bob's friends and relatives chartered a private jet to take him to his mother's house in Miami. His lawyer Diane Jobson bought him a nice suit of clothes, so he would at least look the best possible if anyone chanced to see or photograph him. As they prepared to board, German customs officials pressed him for autographs. Almost too frail to hold the pen, Bob nonetheless complied.

On the trip across the Atlantic, lightning ripped through dark clouds. Bob told his mother he wished he could rise to the window and see it. He had always loved lightning.

Bob had resisted making a will to the last. In times of misery, he had expressed less than charitable sentiments about those he thought were competing for his possessions and money after he died. "Make dem kill demselves over it," someone later told his mother he had said. With time running out, though, he called his attorney in New York and made him promise to see that his family received the rights to his songs.

As he approached the end, Bob tried to comfort his family. "Maddah, don' cry," he told Cedella. "I'll be alright. I'm gwan to prepare a place." He called for his sons Ziggy and Steve. "Money can't buy life," he told Steve. To Ziggy, he said "On your way up, please take me up and on your way down, don't let me down."

Rita, Ziggy (left), and Steven attend Bob's funeral in Kingston, Jamaica. *(Courtesy of AP Images/Ray Fairall)*

On May 11, 1981, just before noon, Bob Marley died. He had lived only two days since returning to the United States. As he had predicted years earlier, he died at age 36.

Bob's body was flown back to Jamaica on May 19, where it lay at the National Arena. The rich and powerful turned out with the poor at the funeral held two days later. Prime Minister Edward Seaga, elected in 1980 to the office he had challenged Michael Manley for throughout the 1970s, gave a eulogy. The Wailers and the I-Threes sang a last time for the man they had accompanied so often on stage. Thousands lined the roads as the body was carried back to a tomb in his boyhood home of Nine Miles.

ten
Survival

In the years following Bob Marley's death, a flurry of albums appeared. The material had come out on previous albums or was culled from rehearsal tapes. But Marley fans demanded more, and record producers obliged them.

Confrontation, released in 1983, contained "Buffalo Soldier," a previously unreleased single about African American soldiers forced to fight in the U.S. wars against Native Americans. It was among the most poignant songs of Marley's prolific career and became another signature anthem. A greatest hits album titled *Legend* followed in 1984. Hardcore fans of any artist tend to regard such collections lightly, but *Legend* has become one of Marley's biggest hits, selling 10 million copies. *Rebel Music* came out in 1986, followed by *Natural Mystic (The Legend Lives On)* in 1995. Boxed CD sets and anthologies continued to pour forth throughout the 1990s and into the twenty-first century.

While his music played on, relations among former band members and business associates deteriorated. The problems grew out of Bob's refusal to prepare a will for an estate estimated at $30 million. Danny Sims, Bob's manager from his days working with Johnny Nash, filed suit claiming Bob had slipped out of a contract he made with Simms in the early 1970s. The original Wailers, Peter Tosh and Bunny Wailer, also waded into the battle, seeking rights to the Tuff Gong label, as did Bob's widow Rita. Rita eventually prevailed in most of the bitter court battles, and today the song rights to Bob Marley's music belong to her company, Rita Marley Music. The royalties go to benefit her and the twelve children, including those she bore Bob, hers by other men, and those Bob had with other lovers.

Ziggy Marley has said he does not care about his late father's money. "Let dem 'ave it, me cyan go out and make me own money," he told reporters. Ziggy formed his own music label, Ghetto Youths Crew, and has released his own albums. The Marley offspring also kept alive the Melody Makers, consisting of Ziggy, Cedella, Sharon, and Steven, begun almost as a lark at the urging of their parents. The Melody Makers succeeded in their own right, releasing the hit album *Conscious Party* in 1988, and following up with *One Bright Day* (1989) and *Jahmekya* (1991).

Rita devotes much money and time attempting to achieve the dreams Bob sang about in his music. She heads The Bob Marley Foundation and The Rita Marley Foundation, which are trying to eradicate poverty in Jamaica and Africa. She helped organize the Africa Unite concert in Addis Ababa, Ethiopia in February of 2005. The concert celebrated Bob's musical legacy and Africa's future, as well as raising money for various charities.

The fates of other Wailers, as well as that of friends and family members, testify to the violence that still reigns among some factions in Jamaica. In early 1987, kidnappers captured and killed the father of Carlton and Aston Barrett. On April 17 of the same year Carlton was murdered in the courtyard of his home in Kingston, shot twice at point blank range. Police charged his wife Albertine and a taxi driver reported to be her lover with the killing.

On September 11, 1987, Peter Tosh was relaxing at home with friends when a gang of three intruders, led by Dennis "Leppo" Lobban, entered his home. Lobban was a street vendor who had done prison time for charges including robbery and assault. He had borrowed money from Peter since the early 1970s. Infuriated when they could not find a cache of money they suspected Tosh had hidden, the gunmen shot and killed Tosh and two other men. Tosh died at age forty-three. Bunny Wailer, who has continued to make albums, lives as a near recluse on his Jamaican farm. He is the last surviving original Wailer.

Tosh's murder was the kind of death Marley himself had often feared, especially since the 1976 attempt on his life, and may have accounted for some of his prolonged absences from his homeland. Instead, long after cancer claimed him, accolades continued to pour down on reggae's best known star.

The Rock and Roll Hall of Fame inducted him in 1994. In 1999, *Time* magazine named *Exodus* its "Album of the Century." In February of 2001 he got a star on the Hollywood Walk of Fame, and the same month was awarded a Grammy

Lifetime Achievement Award. When Rolling Stone selected its "100 Greatest Artists of All Time" in 2004, he came in as number eleven.

In Jamaica, Bob's image and music are everywhere. His face looks down from billboards and adorns everything from t-shirts to liquor bottles. Tribute bands perform covers of his songs in clubs, and he has become one of the driving engines of the island's tourist industry. On what would have been his fiftieth birthday, Jamaica minted a coin in his honor.

His house at 56 Hope Road is now the Bob Marley Museum. Visitors to his childhood home at Nine Miles find not the squalid hovel where he grew up but a rebuilt and embel-lished shrine, enclosed by a chain-link fence. Not far away lies his tomb, where he was buried with mementos of his life, including his beloved ring from Haile Selassie I. His mother Cedella has been known to greet tourists and pilgrims to the site.

The honors that have come since his death would have sur-prised many who in the 1970s considered him just another pop star. The honors might well

Rita touches Bob's star on the Hollywood Walk of Fame. *(Courtesy of AP Images/Michael Caulfield)*

have surprised him too. The Wailers were formed during a time when all of them had to struggle just to stay alive. "We call ourselves de Wailers because we started out cryin,'" he once said. His songs were calls to struggle against poverty, racism, and political injustice, conditions he knew only too well. Not long after being shot, he talked about his songs of oppression. "We mus' fight against the darkness," he said. "It is better to die fightin' for your freedom den to be a prisoner all de days of your life." His songs had helped lift him from poverty, music made people listen to what Bob Marley had to say, and he never doubted its power to make people free.

Bob Marley
1945-1981
*(Courtesy of UrbanImage.tv/56 Hope
Road Music/Adrian Boot)*

Timeline

1945 Born on February 6 in Jamaican village of
Nine Miles.

1962 Records first two songs, "Judge Not" and "Do You
Still Love Me?"

1963 Forms the Wailers, along with childhood friend
Bunny Livingston (later known as Bunny Wailer)
and Peter Tosh.

1964 Wailers score first hit on Jamaican charts, with
"Simmer Down."

1965 Meets soul singer and future wife Rita Anderson.

1966 Marries Anderson; takes first trip to the United States;
lives with mother in Delaware for eight months.

1970 Produces first reggae record, *Soul Rebels*.

1973 Album *Catch a Fire* released in United Kingdom;
Wailers tour England and United States; Tosh
and Livingston leave group.

1974 Makes first album without Tosh and Livingston,
Natty Dread; adds female singers the I-Threes,
composed of wife Rita and soul singers Judy Mowatt
and Marcia Griffiths.

1976 Wounded by a gunman after agreeing to perform at Smile Jamaica Concert in Kingston; electrifies concert crowd despite injuries.

1977 *Exodus* released; tops British charts for fifty-six weeks; diagnosed with melanoma in his right toe; refuses doctor's advice to amputate; skin graft performed and pronounced cured.

1978 Awarded Third World Peace Medal by African delegates to United Nations.

1980 Collapses after suffering a stroke while jogging in New York's Central Park; doctors find cancer in brain, lungs, and stomach; plays last concert, in Pittsburgh.

1981 Dies on May 11 in Miami; buried at Nine Miles.

Sources

CHAPTER ONE: Nine Miles Boy

p. 12, "When me decided . . ." Timothy White, "Bob Marley: All You Need Is Love," *Rolling Stone*, December 28, 1978, 292.

p. 14, "De trut' is . . ." Jon Bradshaw, "The Reggae Way to Salvation," *New York Times Magazine*, August 14, 1977, 24-30.

p. 18, "See all those . . ." Cedella Marley Booker, *Bob Marley, My Son* (New York: Taylor Trade Publishing, 2003) 33.

p. 19, "Auntie Ciddy, everything . . ." Ibid., 55.

CHAPTER TWO: Wailers in Trench town

p. 29, "Why am I . . ." Christopher John Farley, *Before the Legend: The Rise of Bob Marley* (New York: Amistad, 2006), 41.

p. 29, "What about the tradition . . ." Ibid., 47.

p. 34, "He just kept . . ." Ibid., 56.

p. 38, "In de beginnin' . . ." Bradshaw, "The Reggae Way to Salvation," 28.

p. 39, "Here, stretched out . . ." Booker, *Bob Marley*, 89.

p. 40, "He was pretty . . ." Rita Marley with Hettie Jones, *No Woman, No Cry: My Life With Bob Marley* (New York: Hyperion, 2004), 20-21.

CHAPTER THREE: Rastaman

p. 41, "Oh, Beverly, you . . ." Farley, *Before the Legend*, 89.

p. 44, "Look to Africa . . ." Leonard E. Barrett, Sr., *The Rastafarians: Sounds of Cultural Dissonance* (Boston: Beacon Press, 1977), 67.

p. 44, "Princes shall come . . ." Psalm 68:31 (King James Version).

p. 47, "Is a dangerous . . ." Booker, *Bob Marley*, 104.

p. 47, "It come from . . ." Ibid.

p. 48, "Dat wasn't me . . ." Ibid., 109.

p. 49, "Eleanor Rigby died . . ." Official Web site of Seeklyrics catalog, "The Beatles: Eleanor Rigby," http://www.seeklyrics.com/lyrics/Beatles-The/Eleanor-Rigby.html.

p. 49, "Everything too fast . . ." White, "Bob Marley: All You Need Is Love," 207.

CHAPTER FOUR: Cold Journey

p. 55, "livin' in sin," Official Web site of Seeklyrics catalog, "Bend Down Low: Bob Marley," http://www.seeklyrics.com/lyrics/Bob-Marley/Bend-Down-Low.html.

p. 58, "ketch a fire," White, "Bob Marley: All You Need Is Love," 227.

p. 59, "Him se me . . ." Ibid.

p. 61, "We were all . . ." James Henke, *Marley Legend: An Illustrated Life of Bob Marley* (San Francisco: Chronicle Books, 2006), 24.

p. 62, "He's a nice . . . " Farley, *Before the Legend*, 168.

CHAPTER FIVE: The Wailers Catch Fire

p. 66, "They were busted," Farley, *Before the Legend*, 179.

p. 71, "Who set one . . ." White, "Bob Marley: All You Need Is Love," 252.

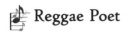

CHAPTER SIX: King of Reggae

p. 76, "Bob needs a . . ." Rita Marley, *No Woman, No Cry*, 101.

p. 76, "It was like . . ." Ibid., 131.

p. 76, "That's why we . . ." Official Web site of Loglar lyrics catalog, "Bob Marley: Burnin and Lootin Tonight," http://www.loglar.com/song.php?id=6940.

p. 77, "where it's at," Henke, *Marley Legend*, 36.

p. 79, "He took it . . . " Rita Marley, *No Woman, No Cry*, 121-122.

p. 80, "Ev'rything's gonna be . . . " Official Web site of LogLar lyrics catalog, "Bob Marley: No Woman, No Cry."

p. 83-84, "Them belly full . . . " Ibid., "Bob Marley: Them Belly Full."

p. 84, "That until the . . . " Ibid., "Bob Marley: War."

CHAPTER SEVEN: Blood for Peace

p. 85, "Bob got shot . . ." Henke, *Marley Legend*, 43.

p. 85-86, "When it was time . . ." Rita Marley, *No Woman, No Cry*, 145.

p. 89, "I jus' wanted to play . . ." White, "Bob Marley: All You Need Is Love," 292.

p. 89, "We find it . . ." Official Web site of Loglar, "Bob Marley: War."

p. 90, "But now he . . ." Rita Marley, *No Woman, No Cry*, 150.

CHAPTER EIGHT: Fame and Scandal

p. 93, "He himself still . . ." Rita Marley, *No Woman, No Cry*, 130.

p. 96, " 'How would I . . ." Ibid., 160.

p. 97, "Next year 1978," White, "Bob Marley: All You Need Is Love," 299.

p. 97, "quite possibly the . . ." Henke, *Marley Legend*, 48.

p. 99, "Me don' wan' . . ." White, "Bob Marley: All You Need is Love," 301.

p. 99, "We got them . . ." Henke, *Marley Legend*, 48.

p. 99, "Babylon by Bus . . ." White, "Bob Marley: All You Need Is Love," 95-98.

p. 100, "And it's the . . . " Official Web site of LogLar, "Bob Marley: Ride Natty Ride."

p. 101, "Don' leave!" White, "Bob Marley: All You Need is Love," 305.

CHAPTER NINE: Fading Light

p. 105, "We can make . . ." White, "Bob Marley: All You Need Is Love," 311.

p. 106, "that a healthy . . ." Ibid.

p. 107, "Who ready fe . . ." Booker, *Bob Marley, My Son*, 177.

p. 109, "Make dem kill . . ." Ibid., 197.

p. 109, "Maddah, don' cry," White, *Bob Marley, My Son*, 313.

p. 109, "Money can't buy . . ." Rita Marley, *No Woman, No Cry*, 168.

p. 109, "On your way . . ." Ibid.

CHAPTER TEN: Survival

p. 112, "Let dem 'ave . . ." White, "Bob Marley: All You Need Is Love," 384.

p. 115, "We call ourselves . . . Ibid., 250.

p. 115, "We mus' fight . . ." Bradshaw, "The Reggae Way to Salvation," 26.

Bibliography

Barrett, Sr., Leonard E. *The Rastafarians: Sounds of Cultural Dissonance.* Boston: Beacon Press, 1988.

Bayer, Marcel. *Jamaica: A Guide to the People, Politics and Culture.* London: Latin American Bureau, 1993.

Booker, Cedella Marley with Anthony C. Winkler. *Bob Marley, My Son.* Lanham, MD: Taylor Trade Publishing, 2003.

Campbell, Horace. *Rasta and Resistance: From Marcus Garvey to Walter Rodney.* Trenton, New Jersey: Africa World Press, Inc, 1987.

Davis, Stephen. *Bob Marley.* Rochester, VT: Schenkman Books, 1990.

Edmonds, Ennis Barrington. *Rastafari: From Outcasts to Culture Bearers.* New York: Oxford University Press, 2003.

Farley, Christopher John. *Before the Legend: The Rise of Bob Marley.* New York: Amistad, 2006.

Henke, James. *Marley Legend: An Illustrated Life of Bob Marley.* San Francisco: Chronicle Books, 2006.

Marley, Rita with Hettie Jones. *No Woman, No Cry: My Life with Bob Marley.* New York: Hyperion, 2004.

Sherlock, Philip, and Hazel Bennett. *The Story of the*

Jamaican People. Kingston, Jamaica: Ian Randle
   Publishers; Princeton: Markus Wiener Publishers, 1998.
Talaman, Bruce, and Roger Steffans. *Bob Marley: Spirit
   Dancer*. New York: Henry Holt, 1992.
White, Timothy. *Catch a Fire: The Life of Bob Marley*.
   New York: Henry Holt and Company, 2000.

Web sites

http://www.bobmarley.com
Everything you always wanted to know about the master of reggae can be found here on the Official Web site of Bob Marley. Among a long list of other things, visitors will find a lengthy and detailed narrative of his life and legacy, photos and biographies of his wife, Rita, and children, videos, an online store, and a link to a community forum, where like-minded lovers of Bob can talk, share thoughts and memories.

http://www.bobmarley-foundation.com
At this Web site you'll find links to The Bob Marley Group of Companies, which comprises a family of affiliated charitable organizations, including The Robert Marley Foundation JA, and the Rita Marley Foundation.

http://www.rockhall.com/inductee/bob-marley
Bob Marley was inducted into the Rock and Roll Hall of Fame in 1994, and this site features an extensive timeline and biography of "reggae's foremost practitioner and emissary."

http://www.thirdfield.com
This Web site bills itself as the ultimate Bob Marley fan site on the Internet, with thirty different sections on the reggae legend, including a thirteen page photo gallery, and an alphabetical listing of all of Marley's lyrics.

Index